THE ROAD TO MARBLE HALLS

The Henry Grammer Saga

by

Arthur Shoemaker

THE ROAD TO MARBLE HALLS

First Edition

**Copyright © 2000 by
Arthur Shoemaker**

**Library of Congress cataloging in
Publication Data**

ISBN # 0-9649790-9-8

Acknowledgments

It is said, "timing is everything" especially when it came to doing research on this book. It has taken several years to pull it all together, and I almost waited too long.

Without the help of C.C. Leuschner (Dogtown Slim), none of this would have been possible. Many, many thanks to Doris Malm of Fort Stockton, Texas for providing the genealogy of the Grammer family. Thanks also to Tom Benbrook of Tucson, Arizona. Many fine Osage County folks, some who are no longer with us, helped on the story; the Walt Colbys, the George Bradens, Alva (Red) Carter, Curt Clymer, Ben (Son) Johnson, Bob Clark and Mark Freeman, Jr. A special thanks to Bill Beaty of Allen, Texas for his insight and stories of his grandfather Pitts Beaty. Jane Pattie of Aledo, Texas is not only a fine writer but had special bond with Dogtown. Also, thanks to Robert K. DeArment for furnishing the story about the shooting in Haskell, Texas.

Lastly, my greatest thank you goes to my wife, Peggy, for sticking with me in the project. She has quit complaining when I need to visit a cemetery or mausoleum for some research.

.

Prologue

The night before he was killed in a tragic automobile accident near Florence, Arizona, Tom Mix and Ed Echols visited in the ranch home of Walt Coburn at his spread in the hills near Tucson. Coburn was, at the time, considered the "King of the Western Pulp Writers". The three men had long been personal friends.

Tom was on his way back to California in an attempt to revive his fading motion picture career after spending several years on the road with his own circus. Echols, at the time, was Sheriff of Pima County, Arizona. Many years later, Coburn, in a magazine article, wrote about the afternoon the three man spent together.

"Following our evening meal and a tour of the ranch, certainly not big by some standards, we relaxed on the long, spacious verandah and enjoyed some smokes and good Mexican beer. Tom and Ed got to reminiscing about their early days with Wild West shows and the early day rodeo circuit. Both had worked the Miller Brothers 101 Wild West Show. While Tom left the 101 Show and headed for California and motion picture history, Ed followed the rodeo trail where he won the steer roping at the very first Calgary Stampede in 1912. Joking about those early days, they kept bringing up names of men like Bill Pickett, Chet Byers, Sam Garrett, Henry Grammer and Yakima Canutt."

"Tom spoke up, 'It must have been around 1904 that I worked a spring roundup with Henry Grammer. It was for the Circle Diamond outfit near Malta, Montana. John Survant was the wagon boss. We hired out for forty a month and all the beans we could eat. Henry was a damn fine cowhand, knew his horseflesh and, as we know, a great steer roper'.

"Echols agreed and added, 'Henry was a great natural-born steer roper and a pretty fair bronc rider. We were both at that first Calgary Stampede. Guy Weadick, who started it all, brought Henry and a bunch of Oklahoma cowboys up to Canada to help him stage that first rodeo. Can you imagine, I lucked out and took first money away from those guys.'

"Tom went on to say, 'Henry had to spend some time in the Montana pen for shooting a sheepshearer in a Malta Saloon. This guy had been molesting an old man. It was self-defense, but the jury convicted him. I once tried to talk Henry into coming out to California to help me make movies, but he didn't want to.'

Coburn went on to say, "The evening ended on a warm, nostalgic note without knowing if the three of us would ever sit around and chew the fat again. As would have it, Tom Mix, the greatest cowboy movie star of all-time, would die the next day, alone, behind the wheel of a Cord automobile."

Colorful as he was, Tom Mix was quite a braggart. He and Grammer knew one another through their association with the 101. Tom was not in Montana at the same time Henry was there. He did know of the Malta shooting.

"Tom Mix! Sure, I'd heard about him all my life," said C. O. Leuschner who was known in rodeo circles as DogTown Slim. "You see, Henry Grammer was my uncle. My mother Irene was his sister.

"I was still cowboying in the bush country south of San Antonio when I learned that Tom Mix had his vaudeville show at the Majestic Theatre in San Antonio. I bummed a ride up

v

there and headed for the theatre. Didn't have any money so I went around to the stage entrance but this guy wouldn't let me in. I waited around until this well-dressed man showed up and I asked him: "Do you know Tom Mix?" He answered: "Yes, I'm his manager." "Will you tell him that Henry Grammer's nephew is out here and would like to meet him.

"About five minutes later, Tom came to the door and took me to his dressing room. We talked about Uncle Henry and some other things before he asked me if I wanted a job taking his horses, including Tony, to Fort Worth. I did. After he started his circus, I worked for him about a year."

The Henry Grammer Saga
Introduction

It must have been ordained that Henry Grammer was not to die in bed. Toward this end, several factors may have molded his hard-driving, competitive spirit. He was only seven years old when his father was shot down in a Haskell, Texas saloon. Then, at the age of twenty-one, a shooting in a Montana barroom cost him two and a half years in the penitentiary. In January 1910, his Uncle Joe was mysteriously shot and killed on the streets of Checotah, Oklahoma. His younger brother Tom suddenly disappeared from Osage County and according to family history, died of blood poisoning in Pierre, South Dakota.

The Grammer family roots were deep in the black soil of central Texas where Henry was born, but being left fatherless at a young age triggered a wanderlust in Henry which took him to Oklahoma, Montana and rodeo arenas from coast to coast, Canada to South America.

In Osage County, Oklahoma he became a towering figure of legend and controversy whose life and colorful career stretched from the last days of the open range to the very early days of rodeo. With a good horse under him and a rope in his hand, he rode out of the nineteenth century into the tumultuous beginning of the twentieth. He lived long enough to become one of the great steer ropers of all-time and also a major player in the wild, wide-open oil boom, which made the Osage Tribe "the richest tribe on earth".

His death was different from that of most men who had lived a life similar to his. He died with his boots on, it is true, but in his case, death allegedly came from being thrown out of a rolling Cadillac automobile, although it was highly suspected he was dead before the wreck.

A short time after delivering a portrait of Henry Grammer to the Osage County Historical Society Museum in Pawhuska, I was invited to speak at a civic club dinner. Speaking as a historian, I said Osage County was a gold mine for good stories: outlaws, oil boomtowns, train robberies, etc. Near the end of my presentation, I mentioned my research into the life and times of Henry Grammer with the intent of writing a book. Almost immediately a hand shot up. "How many men did he kill?" I gave an answer based on research. Again the hand went up. "I know this cowboy who has his pistol and it has six notches on it." My response was entirely unsatisfactory, but as I told him, "Why spoil a good story with facts!"

My research has been founded on family letters and pictures, newspaper accounts, periodicals, books plus interviewing people who knew Henry while he was still living. All of this put together reveals a somewhat different picture than that portrayed over the years.

Making up the legend of Henry Grammer were the same factors that go into all legends; a skeleton of truth, fleshed with prejudice, clothed with awe. This book is an attempt to dissect the legend, to extricate the framework of truth from the body of myth and rage of rumor that have grown up around it. His story requires no sensational embellishments. His was an exciting life spanning a month shy of four decades.

DOGTOWN SLIM

His real name was Charles O. (call me C.O.) Leuschner. It was in 1936 when the rodeo cowboys went on strike at the 1936 Boston Rodeo. A document was written and passed around to be signed by the contestants. The cowboys demanded that the purse be doubled and the entrance fees added to each and every event. Any contestant failing to sign this petition will not be permitted to contest, by order of the undersigned. And one of those signatures is that of Dogtown Slim.

This action was the formation of the United Cowboy Turtle Association. It was said the name "Turtles" was attributed to Everett Bowman. He said, probably in jest, that the cowboys ought to be called turtles, since it had taken them so long to form an organization.

How did he get the name Dogtown Slim? This is what he told Jane Pattie, who published his story in <u>The Cattleman</u> magazine:

"The small town of Tilden in McMullen County below San Antonio, Texas, is located in the South Texas brush country. It had been a stage stop on the old road from San Antonio to Laredo, and a supply center for the area's ranches. When the local ranchers

3

came to town on Saturdays, their cow dogs came with them. There were usually more dogs than people, so Tilden was first known as Dogtown.

"It was still a local gathering place in 1932 when noted South Texas horse breeder, George Clegg, took wiry little steer roper Ike Rude to the Tilden rodeo in search of a good roping horse. They arrived just in time to watch a local cowboy, C.O. Leuschner, get down a big, rank steer during the bulldogging contest."

"Things got a little Western", Leuschner recalls. "I threw that steer, but when I finally got to my feet, my clothes were torn half-off and I had a mouthful of dirt and a horn in each hand."

"Later that year, C. O. was in Chicago, Illinois for the rodeo. He was leaning against a lamppost on Madison Ave. when Bob Crosby, Dick Truitt and Ike Rude arrived from the Pendleton rodeo. Ike recognized the lanky cowboy. "This show's going to be a success," he stated. "There's ol' Slim from Dogtown." So C.O. Leuschner was known as Dogtown Slim during the rest of his rodeo career. His specialty was bulldogging and he stayed with it until he broke his back."

There is much more to his story after he left the rodeo arena: horse trainer and breeder, cattle buyer, and all-round nice guy. I first heard of him in a most indirect way. During the time I was digging some preliminary research into the life and times of Henry Grammer, I learned a Pawhuska rancher, Mark Freeman, Jr., was in possession of a horsehair quirt made by Henry Grammer during his prison days. Calling Mr. Freeman, I was graciously invited to come up for a visit. I did and I got to hold the famous quirt. Mark also mentioned a man named C.O. Leuschner who was Grammer's nephew and how to get in touch with him.

What followed was a long, friendly relationship with C.O. We corresponded and talked over the phone. He provided me with much information on the Grammer family. His mother, Irene, was Henry's younger sister and going through a photo album, he showed me many photos, some of which are published here for the first time.

When I visited him in his San Antonio home, he hauled out a large painting of his Uncle Henry, "Aunt

Maggie commissioned this painting," he said, "and I'll send it to you if you will put it in that museum in Pawhuska." I answered, "I will." He did and I did. It can now be seen in the Osage County Historical Museum in Pawhuska.

It must have been in the summer of 1995 when C.O. called to tell me he had been nominated for induction into the Rodeo Hall of Fame located in the National Cowboy Hall of Fame in Oklahoma City. He was excited and pleased. I told him I would be there for the induction.

Later that summer after the votes had been counted, I got this call from him: "Art, I didn't make it. I was told I missed out by one vote." He was disappointed of course, but passed it off like the old cowboy he was. "I was told, my name would come up next year." I said that would be great and I'll be sure to make it.

Finally, in 1996, C.O. Leuschner, ol' Dogtown Slim, was inducted into the Rodeo Hall of Fame, but this time as a deceased member. He fought and lost a four-month battle with cancer and died October 22, 1995 at the age of 82. He was buried in San Antonio, not far from Dogtown.

There's a lot of C.O. in this story about his Uncle Henry, Maggie, the children and his Uncle Tom. There are folks in the Osage who remember C.O. The time he spent in the Osage was filled with bittersweet memories as he tried to put down many of the untruths about Uncle Henry.

In a way, C.O.'s legacy lives on in the First State Bank in Fairfax, Oklahoma. There, up on the wall, hang his spurs, right next to the ones worn by his uncles, Henry and Tom Grammer.

GONE TO TEXAS

The Grammers Move West

Deep in rural Tennessee, Peterson and Martha Grammer were living in Bedford County where their son Joseph Coleman Grammer was born on February 5, 1825. It isn't known when the Grammers left for Texas, but it was probably in that time period between the Texas War of Independence in 1836 and 1845 when Texas was admitted to the Union.

The bond between Tennessee and Texas had been strong. David Crockett had led a band of adventurers from the Volunteer State to Texas to fight and die at the Alamo. Sam Houston, a former governor of Tennessee, played a vital and lasting role in Texas history: General of the victorious Texan army in the struggle for independence; first President of the Republic of Texas; first Governor of the new State of Texas.

The Grammers settled in Anderson County at a small settlement called Fort Houston. It was intended to become the county seat, but in 1840 it was discovered that the little village was two miles off center. Taking the legislature's guideline literally that county seats should be at the center of counties, a new town called Palestine was created to be county seat. Fort

Houston declined and was later called Tennessee Colony.

Joseph Coleman Grammer grew to manhood at Fort Houston and at the age of twenty-two married Sarah Ann Reeves on March 8, 1847. Their first child, born in 1850, was named Andrew Jackson after another famous Tennessean.

Shortly after this, Joseph Grammer began a slow move across Texas from the piney woods in the east, to the black land belt of central Texas, then lastly, to the dry land vistas of west Texas.

The first stop was Limestone County near a small town close to Groesbeck. Seven more children were born: Johanna in 1853, Thomas Lewis in 1855, Darinda in 1858, Alice Johnson in 1861, Joseph Coleman, Jr. in 1864, and twin girls, Georgia and Virginia in 1870.

About 1876, the Grammers moved again, this time, to Mason County where they lived until moving to Midland in 1884. Joseph Grammer owned a blacksmith shop and Sarah ran their boarding house known as the Grammer House. They are both buried in Midland's Fairview Cemetery.

One of the Grammer men who

didn't move was Thomas Lewis. There was this girl in Falls County who caught his eye. Falls County joins Limestone County to the southwest and according to family legend Tom met Amy Watters at a fair at Marlin, the county seat. Amy's family farmed in the north part of Falls County.

Following their courtship and marriage, they apparently continued to live at Marlin. Their first child, a girl, died as an infant and is buried in the Watters-Seay family plot in the Mount Hope Cemetery in Falls County. Other children were: Ida, Henry, Thomas, Jr. and Irene. Henry was born July 20, 1883.

The children were still small when Tom took his family out to Haskell County, Texas and settled on a small spread on the Double Mountain Fork of the Brazos River. Here, according to family legend, Tom was looking after a string of racehorses owned by Tom Trammel, one of the founders of Sweetwater, Texas. Trammel and his partner named Newman, were two of the best-known quarter horse breeders in Texas at that time. The pride of the string was a coal-black stallion called Tin Shine. He was much in demand for breeding.

In 1890, when Amy was three months pregnant, Tom decided to move into Haskell, the county seat, so she could be near a doctor and so the older kids could attend school. He purchased a house and two lots on the edge of town.

One of the favorite gathering places for the men of Haskell was a two-story wooden saloon on the south side of the town square. It was quaintly labeled The Road To Ruin Saloon and would have its share of local excitement.

In his excellent book: George Scarborough: The Life and Death of a Lawman on the Closing Frontier Robert K. DeArment tells of this incident:

"On October 1, 1887, Sheriff George Scarborough was in the saloon when a notorious character named Williams entered. Once jailed by Scarborough, Williams had a score to settle. He attempted to shoot the Sheriff in the back, but Scarborough spotted him in the mirror over the bar and beat Williams to the draw, shooting him dead.

"Two nights later, the saloon was the scene of another shooting. W.M. Carter, while drinking at the bar, accused

14

J.L. Baldwin, one of the owners, of taking Scarborough's side in the dispute and being unfair to Williams. The argument led to guns being pulled. Carter died by Baldwin's gun."

It wasn't until the afternoon of May 27, 1890 that the next shooting took place in the saloon; a shooting which forever altered the lives of the Grammer family. The Haskell Free Press carried the story:

"Tom Grammar (sic) killed. A quarrel between George Mason and a man named Marshall about a horse race was resented by Tom Grammar, who had gone to the Road To Ruin for a drink. Words passed between Ed Carter and Grammar. Grammar cut Carter in the breast with a knife. R.A. Mason protested and Grammar attempted to cut Mason who was behind the counter. Mason reached for his pistol, shot and killed Grammar and was later cleared on the grounds that it was done in self-defense."

Suddenly finding herself a widow with four small children with another on the way, Amy Grammer buried her husband in the Willow Cemetery at Haskell, sold the property and moved back to Falls County where she told a different version into the shooting of her husband. It became a part of family lore:

"Tom stopped by the saloon for a drink as he sometimes did. It was after a horse race that afternoon. He was having a drink at the bar with his friends when this man Mason walked in and shot him in the back. Poor Tom staggered into the street and died under a tree on the courthouse lawn."

Sometime late in 1891, Amy married a man named Charles Moore. To this union, a son named Mack was born. On April 15, 1896, Amy again delivered a baby, a girl, who died the same day. Two days later, Amy died and was buried next to her baby in the Mount Hope Cemetery.

The Grammer children? Irene told her son, C.O. Leuschner, that Grandma Watters took charge and kept them in school and at work on the farm. Ida was the first to leave the nest when she married and moved to Otto, Texas. When Henry was around 15, Irene said he told this Grandma that he was old enough to strike out on his own. He took a job with a man named Foster who had a string of horses and followed the racing circuit throughout south Texas.

Foster needed a jockey and Henry stayed with him until he outgrew the job.

The years before Henry arrived in the Osage Nation are a blank, but it is believed he learned his roping and riding skills working on ranches. Some say he worked for the Kuykendall interests out of Carrizo Springs, Texas or perhaps it was for the Haddens over in Llano County. The next decade would turn out to be wild and wooly for the young cowboy.

BROTHER TOM AND UNCLE JOE

Any story into the life and times of Henry is filled with misinformation, misquotes, speculation, half-truths and mystery. Quite often the name was misspelled - Grammar.

The two Grammer brothers were close and kept in touch with their siblings. Tom was about two years younger than Henry and had a wanderlust while his brother was in the Montana pen. Zack Miller said that Tom Grammer was a better bronc rider than Henry, but wasn't as good a roper.

Another one of the early-day contestants on the rodeo circuit was Milt Hinkle. He became a prolific magazine writer telling of his experiences. In an article published in FRONTIER TIMES he mentions Henry Grammer:

"I first met Henry Grammer in Milwaukee where he was in a riding and roping contest. We were with W.A. Dickey's Circle D Wild West Show when we played in Pabst Park in 1906. When the finals were over in the bucking horse contest, the mighty Henry was the winner. He rode a moon-eyed, big, black mare called Milwaukee Queen. The day he rode her, she was blind, but this did not keep her from bucking. I lucked out and won second place when I rode a horse named Yellow Fever."

Hinkle was right on target as to the time and place of this contest, but he wrote about the wrong Grammer. It was Tom, not Henry. In 1906, Henry was still in the Montana State Penitentiary.

That it was Tom in Milwaukee is supported by a faded postcard/photograph in the Leuschner family album. The picture shows Tom riding the Milwaukee Queen. On the back: "Tom Grammer, Milwaukee, Wisconsin, Circle D, W.W. Show." On another postcard/photo Tom writes: "Me on the roan outlaw at Rapid City, April 10, 1907. Winner of first money in riding contest." This Rapid City contest was a month before Henry was released from prison.

The Mulhall Wild West Show, as it was now called, was booked to show in five cities in about two months in April 1910. With minor changes in personnel, the program was much the same in each city. One act listed on the program was: WRESTLING MATCH WITH WILD STEER - Tom Grammar (sic) wrestling with a 'Mexican Steer'.

"I guess Uncle Tom had been dead about a year before I was born," recalls C.O. Leuschner. "I was always told that the reason he left Osage County was because he was badly cut up in a knife fight. Always heard that he had a temper, but anyway, he had to be rushed to the hospital by a railroad handcar. It was in 1912 that the family learned that Tom had died in St. Mary's Hospital in Pierre, South Dakota from blood poisoning after having a tooth pulled. My mother received a card written by one of the Sisters at the hospital. I don't know where he is buried.

"When I was growing up, the family always referred to him as Uncle Joe as he was actually my mother's Uncle and the brother of my grandpa Tom. He was Joseph Coleman Grammer, Jr. and he was killed somewhere in Oklahoma," said Leuschner. "The story goes that he was sitting on a beer keg whittling on a piece of a stick when this guy shot him."

Fact or fancy? What was this Uncle Joe doing in Oklahoma and why was he shot and killed? The answer to this puzzle began to unravel as I was reading the memoirs of a former Deputy U.S. Marshall named W.F. Jones. It is a series of interviews published in 1937 where Jones tells of his service in the central part of the state beginning in the year 1897. Jones states he worked in an area inhabited by roving gangs of robbers, horse thieves and murderers.

"One such gang was headed by Mac Alford in 1902,' states Jones. "This gang was suspected of killing a man named Spivey and robbing his place. The gang was spotted and Jones was notified. Jones arrested the gang, but they were released for lack of evidence.

"Running free, a bloody feud broke out between Alford and Cicero Davis, a wealthy rancher who was waylaid at his own gate and shot. Alford was arrested for the murder and tried, but again released. A short time later, Alford was shot from ambush. It was suspected that a man named Dunlap was hired by the Davis clan to shoot Alford, but there was no proof.

"Following Oklahoma statehood in 1907, Edward C. Julian was appointed the first County Clerk of McIntosh County at the courthouse in Eufaula. Julian was considered as an enemy by the Davises because of some information he had passed along. Dunlap went to Eufaula to see Julian who was staying at the Eufaula Hotel. Going to the hotel, Dunlap knocked on the door and waited. Julian opened the door and saw Dunlap was armed and reaching for his gun, but Julian was holding his gun and shot Dunlap killing him on the spot. Claiming self-defense, Julian never went to trial."

Continuing his version of this feud, Marshall Jones said, "In the meantime a fellow named Grammer, who belonged to the gang, came to town after Julian with blood in his eye. He rode in one day in 1910, put his horse in Tom Stone's livery stable and said he was going to get even with Julian. As Grammer left the livery going north on the west side of the street, Julian approached on the opposite side. Each grabbed his gun, but Julian fired first and killed Grammer. I arrested Julian, but he was released on bond while awaiting trial."

In describing this shooting after a period of twenty-seven years must have left the old Marshall's memory a bit fuzzy as his version differs greatly from on-the-spot reporting printed in the January 7, 1910 edition of the Indian Journal, printed in Eufaula and the area's leading newspaper.

"On January 4, 1910 on the principal business street of Checotah and in plain view of many people, about 5 o'clock Wednesday afternoon, Ed C. Julian, County Clerk of McIntosh County, shot and killed Joe Grammer, as the latter was sitting on a store box in front of the Checotah Grocery and Implement Company's store, across from where Julian had stood.

"Eight shots were fired by Julian and five of then went true to the mark. Three struck Grammer in the breast a little to the left of the heart and two struck him in the left arm. Grammer dropped over dead without moving from the box on which he was sitting.

"The shooting on Julian's part was deliberate and without any provocation from Grammer, who was sitting quietly with a knife in his hand. Julian's friends, however, claimed that the dead man had threatened to kill his slayer during the day and that was Julian's reason for shooting first. Julian surrendered himself to officers and was placed under arrest."

This is where William L. (Lod) Calohan enters the picture. Lod was Joe Grammer's brother-in-law married to his sister Sarah Alpha. He was a brand inspector for the Texas and Southwestern Cattleraisers Association stationed at the Kansas City stockyards. He was six foot two and bowlegged from years in the saddle and had the reputation of having committed more than 15,000 cattle brands to memory.

To learn the facts behind the shooting of his brother-in-law, Lod contacted J.B. Lucas, an attorney in Checotah. In a letter dated February 3, 1910, Lucas detailed the results of his investigation:

"Joe Grammer was shot without cause and the killing was not justified in any sense. He had come down from Muskogee and was preparing to go home and was waiting for a buggy and driver to take him out.

"On the day of the killing, Joe was walking around town attending to his own business, strictly sober, and talking with friends. Julian came out of the office of Steen and Buford across the street, walked up to Joe and shot without warning. Joe had been sitting on a box whittling with a small Barlow knife and had no thought of having any trouble. He was not armed and did not even see Julian.

"Julian was under the influence of liquor and afraid of his own shadow and thought every stranger his enemy.

About 12 years ago he had accused Cicero Davis and others of burning some hay that belonged to him in the Cherokee Nation and he thought Joe was a friend of Cicero Davis. No one believes this and they have no grounds for this belief.

"Eighteen months ago, Julian killed a party in Eufaula and ever since that time he had been ready to shoot at anything that shows up before him and it seems that he had been excited at the time and he had drunk to excess."

There is no record of the Grammer family having Lawyer Lucas pursue the matter although he may have been present when Julian finally went to trial in September 1910. Julian and his lawyers must have made a convincing story about the shooting being done in self-defense as the jury acquitted him.

Suspecting that not everyone agreed with the jury's verdict, Julian left McIntosh County before the year was out and moved to Westville, over near the Arkansas line. In 1921, he moved to Wainwright, Oklahoma where he died in 1937 at the age of 70.

Joseph Coleman Grammer, Jr. is buried in the Grammer plot in the Fairview Cemetery in Midland along with his parents, his wife Belle and their three sons.

There is, however, one footnote on the legend of Uncle Joe. Leuschner continues his story: "It must have been sometime in the late 1930s when I was introduced to Buck Boren in the lobby of the Gunter Hotel in San Antonio. Sitting there in those soft, leather chairs, we got to talking about different things and I happened to mention Uncle Henry's name. Buck had known him up in the Osage. He then told me about Uncle Joe. It seems that he had once hired him to look after some cattle he owned and was pasturing up near Checotah, Oklahoma.

"Buck's given name was Melvin, but everybody called him Buck. He had, in the early days, driven cattle to the Osage. On one of those trips, he met Blanche Brown whose father was Charles Brown, one-eighth Osage Indian and the only half-breed to ever be elected Principal Chief of the tribe. Right then, Buck decided that between the girl and the grass, he had no reason to return to Texas."

Buck courted and married Blanche and started a beautiful ranch over on the east side of the county.

Buck and Blanche had a daughter named Kathleen who would marry a man named Gene Mullendore who took control of the ranch away from Buck. Buck went back to Texas and never again set foot in Osage County. Mullendore built on what Buck had started and established the famous Cross Bell Ranch.

MALTA MADNESS

Up in the Osage! This was all that needed to be said. Every cowman across the southwest knew what that meant. The fame of the Osage was so widespread that with the coming of spring there was a growing excitement, an awakening, as trainloads of cattle poured in from the mesquite and cactus ranges of south Texas. As the trains arrived day and night, each unloading point became a frenzy of hide and horns.

Before the arrival of railroads across the Osage Reservation, many cattle trains from Texas arrived via the Santa Fe Railroad to giant pens south of Ponca City at White Eagle Station on the west side of the Arkansas River. This is where trainloads of Kuykendall cattle were unloaded and taken across the river to fatten on Osage grass.

Ira Kuydendall had given Henry Grammer a white horse he called Johnny. Henry and Johnny helped push the herd into the shallow waters of the river onto the Osage Reservation. This is when and how Henry got his first look at the land that would mold his life and his destiny. Here is the place where he would make his home and where he would become a legend.

It was around 1901 and Henry

liked what he saw. He decided to stick around and took a job as cowhand for Sylvester Soldani, an Osage rancher and member of the Osage Tribal Council. Soldani had come to the reservation during the tribe's removal from Kansas and controlled extensive acreage on the far west side of the reservation across the river from Kaw City. The two men would become lifelong friends and future business partners, but before that happened, there was a change of plans that will forever remain a mystery in the saga of the Grammer family. How did Henry wind up in Montana?

We need to go back to that shooting of Tom Grammer, Sr. in that Haskell saloon in 1890. What took place after that is based on family stories alone.

"Grandpa Tom had a younger brother we called Uncle Joe who never got over that killing at Haskell and was determined to avenge his brother's killing," said C.O. Leuschner. "Joe talked a cousin, Jack Spears into helping him trail the men involved in the shooting. Jack was the son of his Aunt Joanna California Spears. There must have been three men involved and one was found dead in a boxcar in Louisiana and one found dead in the Arkansas River someplace. However, the third man was in Canada. A man named Mason. I can't prove anything, only what was passed on in the family.

"Uncle Joe must have gone through Ponca City and talked Henry into going with him on a cattle train to Montana. Henry stayed at Malta while Joe crossed the border and supposedly found Mason and shot him."

No records have been found to support Joe Grammer's tale of vengeance so the truth will never be known, but Joe did return to Texas to raise a family. Eventually he again showed up in Oklahoma where he made headlines in 1910. As for Henry, the Montana legend took root.

In 1890, The Bloom Cattle Company sent John Survant from Colorado to Montana to manage the Circle Diamond's northern activities. He was sent north to find new range because of the steady encroachment of agriculture gradually restricting the operations of the great stock outfits of the southwest. Montana, north of the Missouri River, had once been Indian reservations, but was now open to cattle outfits for grazing. Six miles north of

Malta, Survant established his headquarters at what was called Horse Camp Coulee. There was a cabin, a huge cottonwood corral, eight to ten riders, a cook, and all the paraphernalia of a busy camp.

The Circle Diamond ranged cattle from Milk River to the Canadian border and was the largest cattle outfit in that section of Montana. By 1900, range and water were getting scarce and in 1902, the Company secured 12 townships of grazing land across the Canadian line. At the height of their operations, the Company was running as many as 40,000 head of cattle.

One of the wranglers at Horse Camp Coulee was a young Texas cowboy named Henry Grammer. He was between 19 and 20 years old when he started to work for Survant. Friendly and outgoing, he quickly became one of the top hands for the Circle Diamond. Humanitarian qualities were part of John Survant's makeup. In his day he staked many an impoverished cowboy or miner to a grubstake. His word was his bond always.

Malta was typical of the Montana prairie towns of that day. Its one wide, unpaved street ran parallel to the Great

Northern Railroad tracks. By the turn of the century, sheep men had moved onto the range and wool sheds were spread along the tracks as well as cattle pens. Saloons prevailed among the businesses. There was a mercantile store, restaurant, a tiny bank, a brick hotel and the ever-present livery stable. A long line of well-worn, horse-chewed hitching rails stood along bumpy wooden sidewalks.

Wranglers from the Horse Camp often rode to town to relax with a drink and a card game, but on the night of June 17, 1904, things turned ugly for Henry Grammer. Malta's newspaper, The Enterprise carried the story: "On Thursday night shortly before midnight, a shooting occurred in Fox and Powell's Saloon that resulted in the death of C.L. (Leonard) Houghtaling, a man who came here with a Mexican crew of sheep shearers.

"Houghtaling and another man entered the saloon and began abusing an old man over a twenty-five cent piece. Henry Grammer, a cowboy from the Circle Diamond, was in the saloon at the time and told them to 'cut it out and leave the old man alone.' Words passed between Grammer and Houghtaling with Grammer slapping the deceased in the face with his hat. Constable Richards interfered and got things quieted, but Houghtaling started arguing again. He reached around Richards and struck at Grammer with a pocketknife striking him in the forearm just below the right shoulder. Houghtaling threw his hands to his hip as though reaching for a gun. Grammer ran behind the bar, found a pistol and without hesitation fired at Houghtaling. The bullet struck him in the abdomen about three inches to the left of center and came out about three inches to the right of the rectum.

"After being shot, Houghtaling made his way to the Malta House unassisted and lay down on a cot in the office. He expired from the effect of his wound about 11:30 Friday morning.

"Grammer wouldn't surrender to Constable Richards saying he would ride out to the camp and return the next day and surrender to Valley County Sheriff Cosner which he did."

When Henry walked away from the saloon on the evening of the shooting he wasn't aware of the seriousness of Houghtaling's wound. It was only after he turned himself in to the Sheriff that he learned that Houghtaling had died.

The <u>Valley County News</u>

published in Glasgow, carried a report on the shooting in their June 24th issue a week after the shooting:

"The preliminary hearing was held before Justice Brockway. Attorney Hurd representing the defendant, who claimed that Houghtaling had struck at him with a knife, and his testimony was corroborated by a couple of witnesses, but several others who saw the fracas saw no knife in the victim's hand. To prove his assertion, however, Grammer exhibited a scratch on his shoulder that he said was caused by a knife in Houghtaling's hand. In a dying statement to Dr. Clay, Houghtaling said that he had no knife on his person, but he had a nail in his hand when he struck at Grammer. The unfortunate man was about 25 years old and recently came to Malta from Flint, Michigan. Grammer was bound over in the district court and released on $5,000 bail which was furnished by John Survant and Frank Lampman."

Henry's trial was to take place in Glasgow, seventy miles east of Malta. Back in Malta, the upcoming trial split the town between the cowman and the sheep man, with the sheep people being the most vocal. The controversy was bound to promise a well-attended trial.

Henry's trial made bold headlines on the front page of the <u>North Montana Review</u> published in Glasgow: "HENRY GRAMMER GETS THREE YEARS IN PEN."

"The trial came to a close at a late hour last night when the jury returned a verdict of manslaughter and fixed the penalty at three years at hard labor in the penitentiary. To Grammer and his friends, the verdict was a complete surprise as they had confidently hoped for an acquittal or a hung jury at the worst. Some of his admirers even offered odds that he would come clear. To a biased mind the verdict was also a surprise and there were many who thought that Grammer would be a lucky man if he escaped with a life sentence.

"It is said that a prominent Malta man shed a copious flood of tears when the verdict was announced and declared that he would get even with the jury some day."

In sentencing Henry Grammer, Judge Tatten took occasion to express his dissatisfaction with the penalty set by the jury in this case, and he said: "Sometimes one in my position feels rather diffident into too forcibly expressing disapproval of the verdict of the jury, but I think it would be false to myself and false to the state were I to withhold my emphatic disapproval of the penalty fixed in the verdict by the jury in this case. You are either guilty of murder, or you acted in self-defense. How a jury could have reached a verdict of manslaughter is one of the unfathomable things I have heard of. I have heard of a great deal about this case since the jury brought in the verdict, and I should like very much to know that I was misinformed but the source of my information is such as to refute all ideas of that kind. The only knife there on the night of the killing was one in the hands of an old man, and he never left the place he sat in. It is true that Houghtaling carried a weapon for his protection, but he did not have it with him that night at the time you shot him. You know that, and I am informed from reliable sources, you put your character in question before the jury, and the state permitted the evidence without question, whereas, in truth and in fact, as far as my information goes, you ran the town for some time prior to this occurrence, and defied the officers of the law. The state permitted your character to go without blemish, why it was done is more than I can imagine."

This outburst by Judge Tatten, if quoted correctly in the paper, was fueled by information from the sheep crowd, which differed completely from eyewitness accounts going back to the night of the shooting. Also, his remark that Grammer "ran the town" was completely without foundation. He had been with the Circle Diamond for only a few short months and most of that time had been spent on the range. It would be most unlikely for a man like John Survant to put up bail money for one of his cowhands who "ran the town of Malta." Nor would he have hired one of the best lawyers in Montana to defend Henry.

John Survant was a colorful figure whose range of interests included ranching, farming, political affairs, merchandising, publishing, theater operations, and property development. He was Court Clerk of Valley County and would serve as a State Senator from Valley County. He was a founder of St. Mary's Episcopal Church in Malta. He was definitely not a man to allow a cowboy to run his town.

Survant died in 1951 at the age of 87. In January 1962, he was elected to represent the State of Montana in the Hall of Great Westerners in the National Cowboy Hall of Fame and Western Heritage Center in Oklahoma City.

On November 20, 1904, Henry was delivered to the Montana State Penitentiary at Deer Lodge by Valley County Sheriff Cosner. To enter the prison, a key was lowered by rope from the guard in the tower above. After entering the first gate, it was locked and the key returned to the guard above. A second key was then lowered to unlock the gate into the prison compound and then returned to the tower. By the time an inmate passed through this tower, the administration building, the cell house, and into his cell, he had seven doors locked behind him.

Henry was inmate #1680 and his personal history was processed by the admitting clerk. One error was made on the log. His age was written down as 26 rather than the correct age of 21. The record shows birthplace: Texas; occupation: Cowboy; 5'11" tall, 175 lbs., Relatives: Brother, Tom, Sister, Ida Hankins, Otto, Texas; Sister Irene, Grandview, Texas. Dark complexion,

Size 7 shoe, features: slim, gray eyes, black hair, even teeth. Scar on right arm caused by Houghtaling.

The warden at Deer Lodge was Frank Conley, a remarkable man of drive and ambition who took the job in 1890 and utilized convict labor to build the fortress-like prison. He also established an early release system whereby prisoners could earn credits for good conduct and good works. Early in his time at Deer Lodge, Henry learned, as did most of the new prisoners, to braid horsehair bridles and quirts, but once again, he was helped by his old boss, John Survant.

By the late 1890s, approximately one-third of the prisoners worked outside the walls at special camps. The only means of punishment for an unruly inmate was a rapid return to his cell. However, Survant, knowing Henry's skill with horses, contacted Warden Conley suggesting he put his former cowboy to work on Conley's ranch near Deer Lodge. There was no use for Henry to waste his time in a cell.

Taking the suggestion, Conley did use Henry to break horses to be sold. This caused Henry's time to be served rather quickly and on May 29, 1907 after serving two years and six months of his sentence, Henry walked out a free man. There is a story still told by Osage cattlemen that Henry Grammer rode out of Deer Lodge, Montana on a good horse and a new saddle, both gifts of Warden Conley.

No matter how he left Montana, he made a beeline for Oklahoma, arriving in Ponca City via the Santa Fe. Interviewed before he died in 1988 at the age of 95, Curtis Clymer, early day Osage County rancher, told this story:

"Henry Grammer was a good roper and a decent sort of a fellow. My father, Simon Clymer, was at the Ponca City depot when Henry Grammer got off the train from Montana. He had known Henry back in Llano County. They both must have come up to the Osage about the same time, but my father was a tad older. Henry wanted to get a room and invited Dad to join him for a drink. Henry started talking about being in Montana. 'Simon, when those sheep people learned I was a cowboy, I thought I was as good as hung.' He gave my father a horsehair quirt he had made in prison."

Henry Grammer – Dewey, OK   1912

Dogtown Slim - Colorado State Fair - 1935

Tom Grammer – Zack Mulhall Wild West Show

TOM GRAMMER
ROPED AND TIED IN 51¾ SECONDS
AT PAWHUSKA OKLA
W.T. BOAG PHOTO

Tom Grammer – Carter Race Track - 1910

**Henry Grammer – standing at right
Ponca City**

Malta, Montana

Mr. & Mrs. Henry Grammer
July 10,1907

Henry Grammer & Charlie Farra – Dewey, Oklahoma
July 4,1913

54

Henry Grammer – Dewey, Oklahoma

Henry Grammer – Carter Race Track – around 1910

**Left to right: Jim Barron, Pitts Beaty,
Henry Grammer, W.K. Hale, John Morris, Bright Drake**

**Maggie in furs in front row, Henry standing behind
Fort Worth Rodeo - 1920**

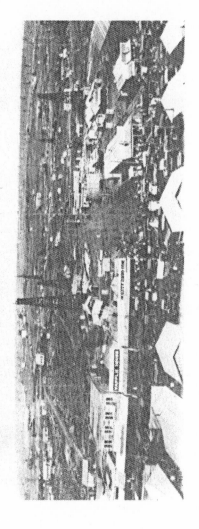

Whizbang in the late 1920's

IOOF Mausoleum – Ponca City
"Marble Halls"

Grammer Crypt
Henry, Maggie, Henry Jr., Tomasine,
Zeke

Henry Grammer
1883 - 1923

Maggie Grammer
1883 - 1965

Henry Grammer in casket

TALL IN THE SADDLE

The Roping Years

By the time Henry returned to Oklahoma, many Osages had received allotments of land on which they were free to live. The whole of the Osage Reservation was the climax of a series of treaties made with the tribe beginning in 1808, 1818 and 1825 where they ceded their claim to most of Missouri, northwestern Arkansas and northeastern Oklahoma. They then accepted a reservation on the Kansas portion of the diminished ancestral lands. In 1865, they agreed to the sale of their Kansas lands and, with that money, the U.S. Government purchased a permanent home for them in Indian Territory from the Cherokees. In 1871-72, they moved from Kansas to what would eventually become the present Osage County, Oklahoma, the largest in the state.

Since the reservation was purchased pursuant to treaty, the Osages were excluded from the General Allotment Act of 1887, and their lands were not allotted until they agreed thereto in 1906. The Act of 1906 allotted the lands of the reservation to members of the tribe in severalty, with each member receiving an average of 658 acres, and reserved all mineral rights to the use and benefit of the tribe.

On the final roll of the 1906 Allotment Act, there were 2,229 enrollees listed. Of that total were 926 full blood and 1,303 mixed blood Osages listed. Each of these enrollees received a pro rata share of the balance of the proceeds from the sale of the Kansas lands and a pro rata share of all mineral income. This would go down in history as a "headright".

The final Osage Tribal Roll was approved on April 11, 1908 and listed every Osage born before that date. Maggie Alexander, born in 1883, is carried on that roll as being one-quarter blood as were her brother Levi, and sisters Ida and Mary. Their father was James Alexander.

Did Henry Grammar know Maggie Alexander before he went to Montana? One can only guess, but it is possible based on the fact that Henry worked for Sylvester Soldani in the same area where the Alexanders had their allotment. But once back in Ponca City, Henry wasted little time in courting Maggie. In just a little over a month after being released from prison, he and Maggie applied for a marriage license at the Kay County Courthouse in Newkirk on July 7, 1907. It shows Henry as 24,

Maggie as 23. Three days later, they were married by Father Renier Seven at the Roman Catholic Church in Ponca City. The ceremony was witnessed by Maggie's brother Levi and niece, Martha.

Maggie was a strikingly pretty bride. In her wedding photograph, she is wearing an empire-style floor-length gown of tucked organza with a high-choke collar, elbow length puffed sleeves with ruffles on the skirt. A floor length tulle veil fastened to a headpiece of flowers.

Henry is standing at her side wearing a dark, single-breasted suit with a boutonnière in his left lapel. Together, they were a most handsome couple. Though Henry's travels took him away from home for extended periods of time, they would remain devoted to each other.

It is believed that Henry took his bride on a honeymoon trip by train to San Antonio with a stop over in Waco and Falls County to visit relatives. Even though she visited Texas many times in later years, Maggie always remembered that first visit to the Alamo City.

Back in Ponca City, the newlyweds rented a house until they

could build a home on Maggie's allotment across the Arkansas River.

"Uncle Henry and Aunt Maggie lived in a two-story frame house trimmed in green," said Leuschner. "I was just a kid but I remember a wide porch on three sides where Aunt Maggie kept her hanging plants. As time went by, Uncle Henry added a barn below a bluff. A long, wooden chute ran from the top of the bluff right into the barn loft. When the children got to be school age, he built an apartment over the garage for their tutor. Later they went to school in Ponca City.

"Uncle Henry brought back a parrot from the trip he took to South America. He fed that bird and talked to it just like it was a child. One freezing winter day, it got out of the house, flew off and froze to death."

The Missouri, Kansas and Texas (Katy) Railroad was the first into the reservation and two Texas cattleman used it to ship some cattle into Hominy where they were off loaded and trailed to the Soldani pens north of Burbank. A veterinarian, Dr. Lewis of Burbank, inspected the herd for ticks and when he found some, quarantined it until they were dipped. Henry Grammer was a tick inspector and made sure the herd was dipped before they were turned out for pasture.

Henry may have been newly married but he wasn't ready to settle down and become a gentleman farmer-rancher. He saddled Old Kid, put on his spurs, coiled his rope and headed for a jackpot roping. One such event made the news in the Pawhuska Peoples Tribune dated September 27, 1907, three months after his wedding:

"Henry Grammer of Kaw City won the $700 prize in Pawhuska in a roping contest over Buck Mathews, the champion Texas roper. They roped 3 steers each, Grammer winning each event. Mathews tied his steers in 130 seconds and Grammer in 112 seconds."

And this was just the beginning. Osage County was a hotbed of roping events and for the next two decades every town in the county sponsored riding and roping contests every spring, summer and autumn. In between, the ropers themselves got together and competed against each other, winner take all.

Steer roping was the hardest of all cowboy attainments and only a handful would truly master the art. A good roper had to have a sense of perfect timing and the ability to judge distance. Calculating the speed of a running steer with that of his horse, he had to judge the amount of rope to span the distance between. Judgment of time and distance was half the battle in good roping. Top ropers seemed to know by intuition the proper time to throw. They were experts who went about the business without any fancy flourishes.

In the beginning, there were not many fancy arenas, just open fields covered with grass, weeds and an occasional corn stalk. "I remember those early days," said Alva (Red) Carter. "We had that old home place out west of Pawhuska a ways where my father built a race track. In fact, folks got to calling it the Carter racetrack. In the middle, nothing fancy, just some high grass and weeds where the fellers did the roping. Guys like Fred Beeson, Blue Gentry, Henry Grammer, Tom Grammer, John Morris, just to name a few who took part in those jackpot ropings."

In 1879, Jacob "Jake" Bartles, a Civil War veteran, settled on the banks of the Caney River south of the Kansas line in Indian Territory. He built a store and water mill that would eventually grow into the City of Bartlesville. After a few years, he sold out and moved his store overland to some farmland he owned several miles north. This new town site he called Dewey, after the naval hero of the Spanish-American War.

In 1908, old Jake decided to host a grand reunion of his old comrades in the Fifth Kansas Cavalry. With his son Joe, he promoted a riding and roping contest for July 3rd, 4th and 5th. It grew and grew attracting the top rodeo hands from all across the west. He would change the name to the Dewey Roundup and it would equal the Cheyenne, Pendleton, Fort Worth, Madison Square Garden and Calgary, Canada rodeos.

Top hands from across the West made it to Dewey year after year; Clay McGonagill, Bill Pickett, Fred Lowry, Fred Beeson, Milt Hinkle, Ben Johnson, Chester Byers and Henry Grammer who made it to Dewey every year but one from 1908 to 1922. The year he died, he had already sent in his entry form.

Why was the Dewey Roundup such a favorite? Just like Henry told the officials at the Frontier Days Celebration Rodeo in Cheyenne, Wyoming, "We boys like to go to Dewey and go for the gold. All you have to do to get it is to win it."

Henry was referring to the colorful practice of Joe Bartles riding out into the middle of the arena after each contest and paying the winners in gold coin.

Paul McGuire, a Pawhuska resident, recalled the first rodeo he saw at Dewey: "Way back in 1916, a kindly neighbor gave me a ride to Dewey, but neglected to give me an admission ticket. I was on my own to get in, so I wandered aimlessly down to the barn where they had the roping horses. I thought I might wander by an open gate and follow a cow pony right into the show.

"The cowboys were cinching saddles, coiling ropes, and taking up a collection for something or other as each of them had a fistful of bills they kept passing one certain fellow and he didn't look like a roper. About halfway to the pens, Ben Johnson rode by, reached down and lifted me up and set me behind Henry Grammer. I told Henry my problem, and in a couple of minutes, I had a grandstand seat and a bottle of red pop. I then saw one of the wildest, roughest, and biggest rodeos that ever happened in this part of the country."

In those early days there were no chutes. The bucking horses were led into the arena and held by a wrangler on a snubbing horse. This meant that the head of the bucker was securely held by the helper as close as possible to the snubbing horse, while men on either side steadied the animal while the blindfold was adjusted over the eyes. Next came the saddle, which was gingerly edged into place and cinched up. If this was not done properly, it could cost the bronc rider his chance at the championship, sometimes even his life.

Henry Grammer, according to Milt Hinkle, was a pretty good bronc rider. At a contest at Dewey, Big Lafe Newman was riding a bronc named Old Paint and got dumped. Henry rode a horse called Dewey and got tossed. The next day, both men switched horses and made good rides much to the amusement of the other contestants. Henry and Lafe got to kidding each other about their bad rides on the first day, so they decided to ride those same horses again. What happened? The same thing as the first day. Henry couldn't ride Dewey and Lafe couldn't ride Old Paint.

For two days in early August 1909, the citizens of oil booming Bartlesville, Oklahoma were treated to a classic contest between twelve of the best steer ropers in the southwest. It was touted to be a contest between Cherokee cowboys vs. Osage cowboys although the ethnic background of the individual ropers had little or nothing to do with tribal bloodlines.

Roping for the Cherokees were: Dwight Barker, Jimmie Rider, Dick Parris, Charley White and brothers, Frank and Dick Watson. Rider and Parris were each early-day pals of Will Rogers.

The Osage team was loaded with fine ropers: Pitts Beaty and John Morris, both former Texas cowboys from the Fairfax area. Beaty was one of the better ropers in Oklahoma and would go on to be a Fairfax civic leader. Morris remained a cowboy all his life and was never seen on the streets of Fairfax without his boots and big hat. Bright Drake was bit older than his teammates, but still a fine roper. Jim Barron was well known on the early-day circuit. Henry Grammer was just reaching his prime and beginning to make his presence known on the circuit. The remaining roper was W.K. Hale, another former Texas cowboy who had settled in the Fairfax area. He never made it big as a steer roper, but did in other ways. In the 1920s, he was deeply involved in the mysterious death of Osage Indians in the Fairfax area.

The two-day event was a rousing success. Thousands attended each day. When it was finally tallied up; the Osage team of ropers beat the Cherokees with John Morris coming up with the best overall time.

Joe Bartles wasn't the only rodeo promoter with whom Henry had a long working relationship. Not far across the Arkansas River in Kay and Noble Counties lay the fabulous 101 Ranch. Quite often, Henry contested in rodeos promoted by the Miller brothers. The 101 Ranch Wild West Show became the proving ground for countless future rodeo champions - both male and female. A number of performers went on to careers in motion pictures: Tom Mix, Jack Hoxie, Hoot Gibson, Art Accord, plus others who played lesser roles.

It was said that Henry could swing his loop clockwise or counter-clockwise and still catch his animal. If this was true, he must have been a sensation when he toured Argentina with the IXL Wild West Show.

According to Milt Hinkle, this tour took place in the winter of 1908 (Nov. & Dec.) and 1909 (Jan. & Feb.). This show was promoted by J. Ellison Carroll and included "Joe Gardner, one of the old-time steer ropers; Henry Grammer, a man who feared neither man nor beast and was a great bronc rider and steer roper; and the wildest cowboy who ever lived, the great Clay McGonagill, bronc rider and steer roper, Tom Grammer, a good bronc rider and Buck Milton, as steer roper and bulldogger." McGonagill and Henry were great friends. It was Clay who named Henry's horse "Flaxie" and considered it to be the best steer roping horse he ever saw. Clay and his wife Annie Laurie often met up with Henry and Maggie as they traveled the circuit. In 1920, Clay was living in Arizona where he was buying and selling horses.

Guy Weadick wrote many years later of Clay's death in 1920: "the roping world was shocked to learn that Clay had come to his end very suddenly. While attending to some work regarding a hay contract on one of the Indian reservations in Arizona, he dismounted from his horse to help the driver of a load of hay remove a live wire that had fallen across the load. The wire was carrying a heavy voltage and, as McGonagill stepped on the steel rim of the wagon wheel and grasped the wire, he received a severe electrical shock which resulted in his death."

Henry was scheduled to judge a rodeo in Fort Worth or he would have gone to Arizona for his friend's funeral. "I remember Clay roping in Muskogee, Oklahoma several years ago. He bet Blue Gentry a thousand dollars that he could rope and tie eleven steers in the same time Gentry could ten. Because of a bad break, it took Clay a minute and thirty-five seconds to tie his first, but Gentry made it in thirty-two seconds. On the next six, McGonagill averaged less that thirty seconds each. And on the eleventh he beat Gentry by seven seconds."

"It was at a little rodeo up in Kansas where Uncle Henry borrowed Blue Gentry's horse," said Leuschner. "He forgot that Blue roped left handed and had his horse trained for this. So when Uncle Henry started after that steer, his loop went one way and the horse the other. Missed completely."

Coming back from South America some of the boys stopped over in St. Louis. Henry went home to see Louis, his new son, while Tom hooked on with the new show Zack Mulhall was putting together. The show opened at the Coliseum. Lucille Mulhall and J. Ellison Carroll put on roping exhibitions. Tom was listed on the program as wrestling a wild, Mexican steer. Maybe it was early day bulldogging.

What happened to Tom Grammer? Just all of a sudden, he wasn't around anymore. Not on the ranch, not even in Osage County.

"We were always told," said Leuschner, "that Uncle Tom got cut up in a knife fight so seriously, that he was rushed to the doctor via a railroad handcar. It was supposed to have happened somewhere around Foraker. It happened at a dance.

"My mother, Irene, got a letter from one of the Sisters at a hospital in Pierre, South Dakota. It was dated 1912 and told about Uncle Tom dying from blood poisoning after having a tooth pulled. I have no idea where he was buried."

This was the same year that Guy

Weadick, Henry's old friend from the 101 Ranch days, promoted the first Calgary Stampede. Weadick had been a trick and fancy roper with the 101 Show but quit and went into other businesses. He called on Henry and Johnnie Mullins to help him in the arena and also be contestants. Henry didn't win the steer roping. The winner was Ed Echols who became Henry's lifelong friend.

"All across Osage County in those early years," said Red Carter, "hardly a weekend went by without some jackpot roping taking place. I recall one at Burbank somewhere around 1915. Burbank was then just a little place east of Ponca City on a branch line of the Santa Fe. It was before the big oil boom. I remember that roping for two reasons: one, Yakima Canutt was in a bloody fistfight with some oilfield tough guy and two, Henry Grammer was stabbed and almost died. The man who knifed him was named Bob Williams."

"I was just a kid," said George Braden, "but I remember that day. The cowboys were standing around that little depot at Burbank when all of a sudden, Henry Grammer spotted this man sitting on a box whittling on a stick. Henry looked him over real good and walked up to him. I heard Henry ask, "Aren't you the hombre who cut up my brother Tom a while back?" Well, before Henry could move, this guy jumped up and stabbed Henry behind the shoulder below the collarbone. He ran off before anyone knew what happened. Henry staggered and fell. He was picked up and stretched out on a baggage wagon. I saw bubbles of blood oozing out of the wound. Luckily, a train was due and Henry was placed on board and sent to a hospital in Arkansas City. He almost lost a lung. Maggie Grammer borrowed $625 dollars from my father to pay the hospital bill. Henry was laid up for a while, but was soon on the road to recovery. Bob Williams was the man who stabbed Henry. The Pawhuska paper named the guy as Tom Quillian."

Henry was as much in demand as an arena judge as he was a contestant, as attested by this article from the Garden City (Kan.) Telegram for Sept. 15, 1916:

"The Cattleman's Carnival was a decidedly clean, fair and open contest in every way. The judges, Mr. Sam Hayes, Mr. George Frey, and Mr. Henry Grammar deserve great credit for the fairness with which they gave their decisions."

Foghorn Clancy, the great early day rodeo announcer, knew them all and remembered Henry Grammer: "Henry was a great cowboy and a fine fellow when he was in a good humor, but he simply could not stand being rubbed the wrong way. He was as fearless a man as I have ever known and odds meant nothing to him in a fight.

"One of his habits was a trick of twisting his neck slightly so as to bring his head sideways as he talked. Friends could judge his temper by the degree his head slanted. There was a tough cowboy in the bronc riding contest at Fort Worth Fat Stock Show and Rodeo. He had a reputation as a fighter and bully. After an afternoon performance, another cowboy told the bully that Henry Grammer has disqualified him on his ride.

"The bully's system was to act so rough that he threw a scare into the judges and they'd give him a higher score than they meant to, just to keep him away. He swaggered up to Grammer in a business manner 'Look here,' he said, 'I understand that you disqualified me on my ride this afternoon, did you?'

'I did,' answered Grammer.

'Why?'

'I disqualified you because you just sat there and never moved a foot. And now that you know I did and why I did, what are you going to do about it?'

'Oh, nothing, I just wanted to be sure.' said the ex-bully as he walked away."

Henry was fully recovered from his knife wound by the middle of 1916 and he and Maggie left the children, Louis and baby Tomasine with relatives and headed for New York to answer the call of his old friend, Guy Weadick.

Having produced successful rodeos in Canada, Weadick had the grandiose plan of promoting one in New York City. Folks in the east were familiar with Wild West Shows, but he wanted to show them how working cowboys from the plains and mountains went about their every day work. There would be no wagon train attacks or stagecoach holdups, but dust eating riding and roping. It was held at Sheepshead Bay Speedway in Brooklyn, New York.

The call went out all across the west. Weadick wanted to assemble the world's finest cowboy and cowgirl talent to show the general public in the east what rodeo was all about. The prize money was to be more than had ever been offered in a cowboy contest anywhere in the world.

The best of the west made it to New York. Riders, ropers, trick riders, bulldoggers, etc. One day former President Theodore Roosevelt attended, as did Will Rogers, who was appearing in the Ziegfeld Follies on the roof of the New Amsterdam Theatre. On the last night of the Stampede, Will invited the whole bunch to be his guests at the show. It was a great night all around.

And, too, the Raceway in Brooklyn was not far from Coney Island where the rodeo crowd spent a lot of time and money enjoying the rides, food and sideshows. In more ways than one, they left their indelible mark on the venerable old amusement park.

On the final day, Emery LaGrande was declared World Champion bronc rider and Ed Lindsey, World Champion Bulldogger, although Iron Mike Hasting had a one-day record of twelve seconds flat and Chet Byers was Champion Fancy Roper. World Champion Steer Roper was Henry Grammer; second, Fred Beeson; third, Clay McGonagill.

Foghorn Clancy wrote: "Guy Weadick's classic event was a financial failure, it ran too long. The contestants received only a portion of their winnings. Otherwise, the Stampede was a milestone in rodeo history. It was destined to be a forerunner of the World Champion Rodeos in Madison Square Garden".

"Uncle Henry got a gold medal stating he was World Champion Steer Roper at that New York Stampede," remembered C.O. Leuschner. "He was proud of it and wore it a lot. Many years later, I asked Tomasine if I could have it, but she told me it was lost."

The hot dusty summer of 1919 was winding down with a September rodeo in Fairfax. The oil boom was going full blast and money was flowing freely and people wanted excitement. This particular rodeo was memorable for two things that took place that afternoon.

Bill Pickett was over from the 101 Ranch to do some bulldogging. The steer he was to take on was a big 900-pound brute that had a sixty-foot head start before Bill broke out of the chute. Gaining ground rapidly, Bill made his jump but the steer fell awkwardly and broke its neck. Bill declined to continue and went hone.

What took place next overshadowed anything that had gone before, when it was announced that a jackpot roping would take place between Henry Grammer and Ben Johnson for a purse of $1000 dollars, some reports say $10,000.

Bob Clark, Fairfax banker, witnessed the contest: "I saw Henry sucking on the knuckle of his ring finger, pull it off and cover a bet. Money was flowing hot and heavy between supporters of each man."

Ben was about 13 years younger than Henry and was coming on strong that summer and was at the top of his form. He would go on and be victorious at the Cheyenne Frontier Days and win the steer roping three times - 1922, 1923 and 1926. In 1927, at Pendleton, Oregon, he roped, tripped, and tied three steers in an average of 18 seconds.

Henry and Ben knew the rules: rope, trip and tie three steers each. The man with the lowest average time was the winner. With a toss of the coin, Ben went first. Unfortunately, a record of the time for each man has been lost to history, but it is a fact that Ben had Henry beaten on his first two steers, so all he needed was a clean trip and tie on the last one to carry home the money.

Johnson's supporters were already mentally counting their winnings when he made a clean throw on the last steer. But when it hit the end of the rope, it broke. It was unfortunate, but all Henry needed to do was catch and tie his steer to win the money. He didn't miss!

Henry's fame as a roper went before him and every promoter, large or small, wanted him in their rodeo. One example of this was an advertisement in the <u>Hominy News</u> for a 1916 rodeo. Contestants: Eddie Burgess, Frank Watson of Wynona, Ben Johnson, Fred Beeson, George Weir and numerous others, but the name Henry Grammer was in bold print. Incidentally, Eddie Burgess was the first fatality in a contest at Cheyenne Frontier Days.

"In those days," explained Red Carter, "the ropers would hire some young guy to trail horses from one roping to another. He could take the string cross-country and take his time getting to the next town. This way, the roper wouldn't be riding his favorite roping horse. I can remember seeing Henry Grammer riding in a buggy with his wife and anyone else who wanted to go along.   Riding cross-country from Pawhuska to Dewey, I had to open fifteen gates.

"We would loan our gear to somebody down on his luck. I've seen Henry pay the entry fee for guys who needed a boost. He was surely generous in many ways."

From Cheyenne, Calgary, Pendleton to Dewey, they were daring, robust, yet chivalrous and romantic. They loved the wild lives they lived.

THE RIDE TO
VALHALLA

By the first of December 1919, the days were bitterly cold in Ponca City and the city seemed to be slumbering in a peaceful, law-abiding manner looking forward to the Christmas season. The city was booming, prosperous and, with a new, growing Marland Oil Refinery, called itself, the "Queen City of Northern Oklahoma". And just across the river in Osage County, oil activity would gain a gigantic boom unprecedented since the first well was drilled in the 1890s. Much of this increased wealth would find its way to Ponca City.

The quiet of a December night in 1919 was broken by a shooting in the Leland Hotel in Ponca City. As carried in the December 9th edition of the Ponca City News: "About seven o'clock Monday evening, Harry Church, nicknamed "Pony", lies wounded today, his right shoulder shattered by a thirty-eight caliber in the hands of Henry Grammer, an Osage ranchman. At press time, Grammer had not been apprehended.

"Just what brought about the shooting may never be fully explained. Dozens of conflicting stories were passed about the city with regard to the affair today, but none of these could be verified. The story was that Grammer shot Church after the latter had won the sum of $3,500 from him during a poker game. This story is denied by principals and a thorough investigation by a News representative failed to discover any authentic foundation for it.

"According to witnesses, Grammer was in company with several prominent Poncans who had gathered in a room at the Leland Hotel to discuss a business deal. Apparently Church had been in the room and had gone downstairs. When he came back up to the second story room and opened the door when a shot rang out. Police and a physician were summoned to dress the wound of the injured man. Church had been shot in the arm."

The following day Henry drove to the Kay County Courthouse in Newkirk and surrendered to authorities. He was released after posting a $3000 bond.

George Braden, Osage County rancher, remembered hearing about the Church shooting: "It was rumored about that Henry and Sid Delaplain were in a card game when Church was caught cheating and Delaplain threatened him and went for a gun. For some unexplained reason, Henry took the blame saying he would be accused anyway."

Henry was to have his preliminary hearing before Judge Burke on December 16, 1919, but it was postponed when Church reported that he was unable to attend. The next hearing was set for January 6, 1920. On January 7, 1920, the Ponca City News reported: "The preliminary hearing of the case of Henry Grammer being charged with the wounding of Harry Church was to have been heard yesterday afternoon but due to the illness of members of County Judge Burke's family, the latter agreed to a postponement of the hearing. It is now set to come up in March."

Henry and Maggie took this time off, between court hearings, to take a trip to Fort Worth, Texas to attend the Fat Stock Show and Rodeo sponsored by the Texas and Southwestern Cattleraisers Association. Henry, a member of the Association, was often called on to judge the rodeo.

Before he left for Fort Worth, Henry took time to write a picture-postcard to his sister Irene living in

Marlin, Texas.

"Dear Sister. Just a line to let you know we are well. Maggie and I will attend the Fat Stock Show in Ft. Worth from the 9th till 13th March. You and Charley better come to it. I am one of the Judges there. Will be at Chandler Hotel. Your Bud, Henry."

The picture on the card shows Henry mounted on Flaxie. He wrote on the face of it: "Taken at a roping last fall."

Back on the ranch, Henry kept busy, with his farming activities, plus his combine business with partners Mac Gardner and Sylvester Soldani. If he was off on a roping some place, he had hired hands to do the work.

"Uncle Henry always had a lot of hogs to butcher in the winter time," said Leuschner. "Good thing, too, as Aunt Maggie always had eight to ten people around the dinner table. Uncle Henry was always accommodating when someone needed help, but if he thought someone was cheating him, that was a different story."

Walt Colby remembered when Henry once helped out his father, Bert

Colby: "Henry was driving home from Ponca one day after a rain when he got stuck in a big mud hole close to our place. Dad went and got his tractor and pulled Henry's car back in the road. Apparently, Henry never forgot that favor. Once when we ran out of corn to feed our hogs, Henry heard about it and sent down a big wagonload of corn for us. He said he was just returning a favor to friends."

It was said that before statehood, Ponca City, a wide open cowtown, had fourteen saloons, making it a lively place along with sister city, Kaw City off to the north part of the county - both places, just a short wade across the Arkansas River. After Oklahoma came into the Union as a "dry" state, the open saloons went underground, so to speak. But many creek bottoms in Kay and Osage Counties harbored moonshine stills. And the demand for "white lightning" would soon take off like a rocket.

Oil discoveries were nothing new to the people of Osage County: Avant, Wildhorse, Hominy, Personia, Naval Reserve, etc., but when E. W. Marland drilled in the Bertha Hickman #1, he uncovered the 21st largest oil field in the first half of the 20th century, the prolific Burbank Field. This giant field covered thirty-three square miles and was said to have generated more wealth than all the old West gold rushes combined. The billion-dollar Burbank Field started what one historian called the "great frenzy."

This land was still in its frontier mode. Where thousands of Texas steers once grazed over limestone prairies, growing fat on Big Bluestem grass, there now sprung up crowded little ramshackle towns with colorful names: Carter Nine, Shidler, Webb City, Cooper, Lyman, Apperson, and DeNoya, better known as Whizbang, the wildest of them all. The rush was on! Workers came, many with families. Overnight, wooden buildings shot up; rooming houses, stores, and offices lined the dusty streets that became nearly impassable in wet weather. Trucks and wagons hauled lumber, tin, pipe, tanks - anything necessary to build a derrick or a town.

Along with the honest, mostly single, hard-working oilmen came the riffraff, the hustler, gambler, bootlegger, prostitute, plus ex-convicts who would kill for a price. It was a decade of high rollers who could launder ill-gotten money in the boomtown frenzy and nearby small town banks.

Notorious Whizbang! One old-time driller and tool pusher recalled the wild disorderly times: "the real name of the place was DeNoya, after the Osage family who had the land where the town sprung up. The place had no city government, no mayor, no council, no nothin'. Dope addicts could easily get narcotics, and booze was plentiful. Some of the first lawmen up and down the Burbank field were Jazz Bo Thompson, his brother Snake Thompson and a tough gunman turned lawman named Jose Alvarado. Law and order was slow in coming, but after many killings, shootouts, and disappearances, most serious crimes were brought under control."

During the 1920s, in order to police the vast area of Osage County, the Sheriff was allowed only one Under Sheriff and two field deputies. The County Attorney was allowed a secretary and one assistant.

One day, before the big fire in Whizbang in December 1923, state officers and oil companies got together and rounded up the dopeys, girls, and other no-goods, and hauled them twenty-five miles north to the Kansas line and dumped them out, but most made it back in a short time.

The 18th Amendment to the United States Constitution was ratified on January 29, 1919. It banned the sale, manufacture and importation of liquor in the United States. Of course, the ban on liquor had been in effect in Oklahoma since statehood. This ban had no bearing on the lucrative bootlegging business near the wide-open boomtowns. Many of the local lawmen merely looked the "other way" and some were later accused of taking money from the bar operators. Many citizens considered the bootlegger as providing a necessary service to the community.

The same lawmen, both county officers and local officers were forced to deal with more serious crimes: murder, holdups, robberies and the like. Bootlegging was considered to be "victimless crime"

Tom Benbrook grew up in the Arkansas River bottoms in Osage County along Charley Creek and vividly remembered the days when moonshine stills operated out in the open: "I remember seeing one 100 bbl. still right out in plain sight. I've seen Charley

Creek, near our home, run white with mash after the 'shine was taken off. Our cow pasture joined the Grammer pasture to the north. In the corner of his pasture was a still and I heard a man named Ballew was making whiskey for Grammer."

"I don't know why Henry went into the whiskey business," remarked Walt Colby. The Colbys and the Grammers were neighbors and knew them well. "I went to school in Ponca City with Louis, the oldest Grammer boy. Maggie was getting good money from her headright and Henry still made money roping and ranching, but I guess he saw a challenge and got into that business. He wasn't the only one. It was a tough business and took tough men to run it. Henry never did anything half way."

"There was one winter, can't remember the year, but we were practically snowed in," said George Braden. "We weren't alone in that respect. All the ranches were snowed in. One morning, we saw a car plowing through the snow up to our ranch house. It was Wetump Tindle, one of Henry's men. He said Henry was delivering a quart of his best whiskey to every family snowed in. The whiskey was to be used to ward off colds and chills."

There used to be a saying that when a cowboy reached the age at which he could no longer flank a calf or ride a bucker and stick to the saddle, he followed the march of progress that robbed him of both these activities. And that meant when the aches and injuries began to mount up, the old cowboy slowed up.

Whether or not this had any bearing on Henry getting into the whiskey business or he simply saw it a business venture that could yield a sizable profit, no one can say. However, he called on his family for help. His sister Irene, her husband Charles Leuschner and their two children were still living in Marlin, Texas. Henry moved them to Osage County and settled them on a ranch about a mile from his place.

"My father was a business man and a perfectionist with figures," said C.O. Leuschner. "He could figure interest in his head faster than most people with a pencil. He had been in the mercantile and grocery business in Falls County, but because Uncle Henry, often away at some rodeo, needed help, my parents conceded to move to Osage County. It must have been around 1920. My sister and me started to a little school house on Charley Creek."

While still awaiting the outcome of his pending trial for the Church shooting, Henry was involved in another shooting. And again, like that long ago shooting in Montana, it was done in self-defense. Tragically, the victim was a close acquaintance.

What happened on the night of the shooting is subject to much debate. This account was printed in <u>Tragedies of the Osage Hills</u>: "Henry Grammer shot and killed Jim Berry about ten o'clock Saturday night, August 7, 1920 at the former's ranch in the northwestern part of the Osage Reservation. Grammer is a well-known cowboy throughout this section and at one time was Champion roper of the world.

"Immediately following the shooting, Grammer, accompanied by his wife and children walked to the home of John Newman about a quarter of a mile away and phoned to some neighbors that he killed a man and that he wished to come over. Grammer and Newman then got into Newman's car and drove to Kaw City from which place he phoned the Sheriff's office in Pawhuska asking someone to come out. In the absence of the sheriff, Deputy Dempsy Smith and his son, Paul, and County Attorney Corbell (sic) Cornett started for the scene thirty-five miles away. They arrived there about 2:00 a.m. and found Berry dead in the same position he assumed when falling from his horse.

"The Grammers, Newman and C.O. Powers, who was an overnight guest at the Grammer's, met the officers when they arrived. According to Grammer's statement, he and his brother-in-law, Andrew Trumbly, had engaged in a dispute in the afternoon over the removal of some cattle that had been grazing in Grammer's pasture. Grammer wanted the grazing fee paid before they were removed. An argument ensued. At the time, Berry was a cowpuncher on Trumbly's place and took no part in the argument. About six o'clock, however, Berry went to Grammer's place and took up the argument for himself, saying he did not like the way Grammer had treated Trumbly. Grammer told him it was none of his business and the best thing he could do was go home. After some persuasion on the part of both Mr. and Mrs. Grammer, Berry left.

"After entertaining their guest with some pictures of former roping contests, everyone retired for the night. A short time later, a voice called "Hello!" Grammer asked what was wanted? It was Berry who had ridden up on his horse and yelled for Grammer to come out. Henry, expecting trouble, took his .45 along and went out in his nightclothes. When they were about thirty feet apart, Berry fired on Grammer who fired back. Berry's horse turned and started down the road. The horse walked but a short distance when Berry fell to the ground and was found dead. No one touched the body before the officers arrived. On examination of Berry's gun, it showed it had been fired twice. It was a .38 on a .45 frame."

"I can hear my mother now telling the story about this shooting," said Leuschner. "Uncle Henry and Jim Berry were friends and this shooting really tore him up. The way I heard it was that Berry was drunk and wanted to get even with Uncle Henry. Everyone was in bed when Berry rode up on his horse and called out and fired one shot at the house. Henry went out on the porch

103

and asked who it was and Berry shot again. This is when Henry shot. He held his fire as Berry's horse turned and walked up the road. He thought Berry was leaving, but he fell off his horse."

Henry volunteered to return to Pawhuska with the officers and was held in the jail overnight. At his arraignment the following morning, some of his close friends were in the courthouse with him.

"Henry asked Barton and me if we could go his bail," said Red Carter. "We were ready to put up a piece of property to cover the bail, but when he heard the bail had been reduced to $2,500, he stopped us and said 'Hell! I've got that much in my wallet'."

The Tuesday following the shooting, Henry's preliminary trial was held at the Osage County Courthouse. After hearing from eyewitnesses, Henry was not charged. The Court determined that since there were adults and children in the home and they were in danger of the random shot fired by Berry, it was clearly a case of self-defense.

"One of the last times I visited with Henry, said Red Carter, he said, 'Red, my reputation has been laid on me by others and exaggerated until I've sometime had trouble recognizing who they're talking about'."

Back in Kay County, Henry was still under indictment for the wounding of Harry Church. Finally, after many delays, he was brought to trial on November 23, 1920 and was acquitted by the jury. The long wait was over and it shattered a myth often told following his death. As the story went, the Federal authorities were holding Henry on some bogus charge when the rodeo officials at Fort Worth asked that Henry be released so he could judge the bucking horse contest. If this could be arranged, Grammer promised to return to jail.

This same story printed after his death stated that Grammer was a suspect in a Coffeyville bank robbery around 1915 or 16. This happened as Henry was recovering from his stab wound. Following the Dalton's failure as bank robbers, there was not an attempted bank robbery after that in Coffeyville.

These statements made for colorful reading, but were definitely not true. They only added to the Grammer legend.

"A lot of the things I remember about Uncle Henry didn't take hold until mother talked about him," recalled Leuschner. "He was a good business man with a pretty good education from those years in Falls County. All the Grammer kids were pretty smart, even poor old Uncle Tom. I wish I could have known him."

The shooting of Jim Berry and the trial for the Church affair took its toll on Henry. He needed to get away for a while so he left the older children in school and took Maggie and Buster to Hot Springs, Arkansas.

Filed away in the Leuschner family album is a picture postcard showing Maggie and Buster riding in a little cart pulled by a goat. It was mailed from Hot Springs on Dec. 1, 1920:

"Dear Irene and All. Are leaving for home Sunday. Henry is much better. Write to us soon. Love to all, Maggie and Buster."

By the time the Grammers had returned home to spend the Christmas holidays, change was under way. The tall grass prairie that first drew Henry to the Osage was becoming a melting pot of humanity. Thousands of people were moving in cutting deep ruts on the land, hauling drilling rigs, building wooden derricks and tanks. Close behind came the little towns that sprang up like mushrooms after a rain.

It was easy to get caught up in the excitement of the times where everything pulsed twenty-four hours a day. One wag said, "Whizbang is where they whizzed all day and banged all night." Many men had worked in earlier booms: Glenpool, Drumright, Three Sands, Ranger, Healdton and would drift on to Seminole, Cromwell, Oklahoma City and the gigantic East Texas field.

Contrary to popular belief, there was not enough corn grown in Osage County to make enough homegrown whiskey to supply the demand. According to the County Attorney Charles Roff: "A goodly number of stills were found and destroyed, but a lot of the moonshine came from the corn growing counties from other parts of the state: Grady, Coalgate, McClain, Okfuskee, etc. The real stuff, like bottle-in-bond whiskey trickled down all the way from Canada. Much of Grammer's reputation as a major whiskey supplier was mostly rumor and spread about after his death."

Roff cites one example of a law enforcement raid aimed at Grammer's moonshine activities: "As County Attorney, I was invited to participate in what was to be a giant raid in the western part of Osage County and this raid was to be carried out by the State Attorney General's office in Oklahoma City. The arrests were to be made by Prohibition officers for the State and the Osage Agency.

"The raiding party gathered in Newkirk, County Seat of Kay County and the search warrants were written by a Justice of the Peace from Osage County. The first stop for the raiders was to be the Grammer Ranch.

"The raiders were led by a small-time oilfield crook named "Smokey" England who said he knew exactly where Grammer hid his booze. Henry wasn't at home when we arrived so the warrant was served on Maggie.

"Smokey led us first to the barn. Nothing was found. There were no hidden cellars, no false walls, nothing. Some of the officers were so irritated at Smokey that they kept poking him in the stomach with their rifles threatening to shoot him. It finally dawned on us that England had probably not ever set foot on the Grammer Ranch.

"We next went to a ranch house run by someone said to be kin to Henry. (Roff didn't know the relationship). No one was at home, but we found a cistern full of gallon jugs containing corn whiskey. The prohibition men destroyed most of the jugs, but confiscated a fair number to hold for "evidence". Much of this "evidence" never made it to the courthouse. It was prime "shine".

"As an aftermath to this raid, there was some publicity which no one expected, every person on the raid was subpoenaed to appear in the federal court at Guthrie, where charges had been filed against the occupant of the raided premises, who turned out to be a nephew (sic) of Henry Grammer. At the outset of the trial, the defendant's attorney raised the question of the legality of the search warrant. When Judge Cotteral heard that the warrant had been issued by an Osage County J.P. while in Kay County, and that the premises described to be searched was actually the Ballew Ranch, four miles away from the raided ranch, he dismissed the case.

"He then ordered all of us raiders to line up in front of the Bench and gave us a lengthy and scathing lecture about law enforcement. It appeared that a rifle and a camera had also disappeared from the home. I knew nothing about that, but I did make and eat two delicious sandwiches from the ham that had been left on the dining table."

Even before this big raid, which took place in May 1923, an ever-darkening cloud was hanging over the Osage Reservation. Roughly beginning around 1920, certain Osage Indians were dying mysteriously. Poisoned whiskey was suspected for many deaths, outright murders soon followed. This period of time would soon be publicized as the Osage Reign of Terror and would center on a one-time steer roping buddy of Henry's.

It was once said better if oil had not been discovered in the county, if, instead the Osage were as poor as the Pawnees or the Otoes, as poor as the white man had intended them to be after moving them off fertile Kansas lands into the sandrock, blackjack hills and prairies, not knowing the land floated on a sea of oil.

The Osage is a beautiful land, as anyone who has wandered over its vastness can agree. Its lush pastures, early on, provided the only area where carloads upon carload of cattle were shipped in each year for finishing, without the need for supplementary feed.

Oil discoveries moved steadily across the Reservation from the east to the west. These oil strikes on the Reservation brought great wealth to both the Osages and the oil companies doing the drilling and refining. All of this activity created boomtowns which faced the same conditions that had confronted Dodge City in the days of the cattle drives, gold-mining Tombstone, any of the wild reckless boomtowns famed in Western Americana; Virginia City, Deadwood and all the rest.

The difference was that the Osage was viewed in the limelight of mass communications. Other western boomtowns had been viewed in retrospect. The nation became aware of Tombstone's and Virginia City's wickedness and violence long after those wild old places had been tamed. The blood and thunder in the Osage was happening now. The nation was astonished, shocked, and secretly delighted to find an outpost of the Old West still alive, "raising hell and putting a chunk under it". It made for avid reading, boosted newspaper circulation, and brought forth howls of condemnation from the righteous.

An example: Where else but in the Osage Nation would Oklahoma's last train robbery have taken place. It was

August 1923 when Al Spencer and his gang robbed the Missouri-Kansas-Texas (Katy) Limited as it was pulling away from the tiny town of Okesa, a few miles west of Bartlesville. In screaming headlines, Spencer was already known as the "Terror of the Tri-state Area". Along with robbing banks, he once robbed the Pawhuska post office. He was truly one of the last outlaws who made the transition from stirrups to steering wheels.

One of the train robbers with Spencer at Okesa was a balding man by the name of Frank Nash. The two had become acquainted while serving time at the Oklahoma State Penitentiary. Nash, whose checkered criminal career would be the catalyst leading to the infamous Kansas City Union Station Massacre in 1933.

In Fairfax, where cowboys in spurs and big hats mingle with Osages in their colorful blankets and shawls, business establishments never closed their doors. It was May 1921 and the talk going around was that the body of Anna Brown was found, badly decomposed, near the Fairfax-Pawhuska road. She was the youngest daughter of Lizzie Q and sister of Mollie Burkhart and Rita Smith. While a crude and hasty autopsy was being performed, a single bullet hole was found at the top of the skull.   There were suspects, but her murder remained a mystery.

Henry Roan, also known as Henry Roan Horse, was Anna Brown's cousin. He was found shot in the head and left slumped in his car northwest of Fairfax. It was about ten days before the body was found. An inquest was held, but no evidence was developed.

On the night of March 9, 1923, a terrific explosion rocked the town. When the dust cleared it was learned it was the home of Bill Smith and his wife Rita. Smith and Rita were dead along with their servant Nettie Brookshire. Rita was daughter of Lizzie Q and Anna Brown's sister.

There are others who died mysteriously: Charles Whitehorn, Joe Yellow Horse, Bill Stetson, Lizzie Q, mother of Anna Brown, Rita Smith and Mollie Burkhart. Barney McBride, an oilman and friend of the Osages, volunteered to travel to Washington, D.C. to ask for a government investigation. He was found dead near Meadows, Maryland. George Bigheart and his attorney, W.W. Vaughn both died under strange circumstances.

This period of time, 1920 to 1926 made great fodder for the news media and has, over the years, furnished material for countless books. One author stated, "Writing about the murders is a cottage industry in Osage County".

Nearly forgotten in all the frenzy was another aspect of life in the financial affairs of the Osages. Certificates of competency were issued to Indians who were deemed capable of handling their own financial affairs, and the recipients of these certificates could dispose of their headrights and property as they saw fit. Osages considered incompetent had to have a guardian appointed to guide them in their financial transactions. This spawned a system of fraud and corruption through which many of the Osages were swindled out of their land and headrights by guardians in conspiracy with merchants, auto dealers, etc.

This guardianship system was controversial and many ugly stories circulated on the numerous ways swindlers operated within a murder ring to siphon off the Osage money.

Charles Roff wrote in his book A Boomtown Lawyer in the Osage: "To my mind, one of the most insidious causes of the lack of concern for law enforcement or the spirit of "I don't want to be involved" was the guardian system of the Osages. At the application of the Osage Indian Agency, many if not the majority members of the tribe were adjudged by the county court to be incompetent to handle their own affairs. Under the law, a person could be the guardian of only five Indians, but this provision was circumvented especially by some lawyers, who had their secretaries and other employees appointed guardians and thus controlled the financial affairs of three or four times the legal number. The guardian not only determined what the ward could buy, but where he could buy it. It was a general practice to add 10 to 15 percent to the selling price as a kickback to the guardian. I cannot help believe that such flagrant cheating of the Osages tended to create an indifferent or callous attitude toward law enforcement except for the most serious offenses such as murder and bank robbery."

The wild race for oil riches in the far-flung Burbank Field was going at full-throttle. Until local operators could get their stills set up, moonshine was coming in from outside the county. The corn growing counties of central Oklahoma provided much of the moonshine until it was easier to ship carloads of corn in by rail.

Henry Grammer saw this illegal whiskey business and considered it a challenge, so he provided the backing for men to operate the still and he would buy the output and sell it to distributors. Competition was stiff and often led to random hijacking of deliveries. One such hijacking led to screaming headlines in February 1923: "HENRY GRAMMER SHOOTS AGAIN."

The gist of the story was that a man named R.N. "Red" Jacobs was delivered to the Pawhuska Hospital by ambulance and was suffering from a bullet wound to his buttocks and his clothes full of bullet holes. He was drunk and telling the hospital staff that he was shot by Henry Grammer. He kept repeating: "I'm going to die." The next morning, sober and realizing he was going to live, he recanted his story of the previous night. He admitted he didn't know who shot him.

This shooting had taken place south of Pawhuska at the residence of a woman named Jessie Findley. Everyone knew her place where men could relax and drink fine whiskey. It was said that she sold only to her friends and apparently she had no enemies.

On the night Jacobs was shot, he had just delivered a case of fine Canadian whiskey to Findley's place. It was as he was leaving her place when he was shot and wounded. Findley called the ambulance.

For seventy-five years, it was believed that Henry Grammer had indeed "shot again". After all, he was that kind of man; "quick on the trigger'. It added to the Grammer legend.

It wasn't until 1927, after he was no longer County Attorney, that Charles Roff heard the true story behind the shooting of Red Jacobs. He was in Ponca City enjoying a Thanksgiving Day meal with Fred (Wetump) Tindel and his wife, Hazel. Wetump had worked for Henry and they were good friends. Wetump told this tale to Roff:

"The afternoon of that shooting, Henry got a call from Red Jacobs who ordered a case of Canadian whiskey and wanted it delivered to Timber Hill west of Pawhuska. Henry got this kid, who did odd jobs for him, and told him to make the delivery. When he got to Timber Hill, he met Jacobs and a man named Bob Young. Jacobs pulled a gun and shot the heel off the kid's boot, took the whiskey and headed for Pawhuska. Jacobs stole the booze.

"When this kid got back to Henry's place, he was scared and told Henry the whole story. Henry was furious, not so much at losing the whiskey, but the kid could have been hurt. He called Jessie Findley and asked her to call Jacobs and order a case of Canadian whiskey to be delivered that night to her place.

"Henry and me drove to Findley's and arrived after dark. Soon Jacobs arrived, but didn't see us. We watched him leave the whiskey with Jessie and turned around to leave. I got out of the car with a pistol in my hand. At my first shot, he turned and ran. I fired six more times before he fell to the ground. Charley, I thought I was hitting him, but only hit him in the butt with the last shot. Henry never got out of the car."

By 1922 and 1923, the investigations of the Osage murders

were still in their infancy. Everything seemed to be centered in the Fairfax area and pointed to certain prominent citizens and some who were not so prominent. These ongoing investigations would soon evolve into years of bitter infighting between the Federal, State, and County governments. This would last for years and most unusual methods were used to gain convictions.

While all of this was going on, the boomtowns were booming as wildly as ever, even more so and drilling was growing daily. The illegal whiskey business was also growing daily. Grammer still had some men operating stills, but he was not the only one doing this. It was doubtful that he was the "true" kingpin of the boomtown whiskey business, although he was given that title.

Adding to the daily tragedy of life and death that played out their run in these wild booming times were those who dared to play a part of this last hurrah. So many workers rushed into the far-flung towns, they quickly overcrowded all existing accommodations. They slept anywhere they could. If one was fortunate to have a room, he often shared a bed.

Catering to the workers were hoards of camp followers. Many local residents deserted nearby farms to open "mom and pop" cafes and other businesses. Others were less law-abiding. Some towns like Whizbang were a mecca for prostitutes, bootleggers, gamblers, con men, thieves, hijackers and a multitude of other less desirables who sought to separate the honest worker from his hard earned money. Isolated drilling rigs were frequent targets for hijackers and robberies were common.

Contributing to the problem of vice and violence was the absence of established government in many towns. Liquor had long been banned on the Osage Reservation and throughout Oklahoma following statehood, but this had little effect on liquor sales or the consumption of the same. Overwhelmed by this constantly moving mass of people, most Osage County lawmen viewed bootlegging as a victimless crime. In fact, the bootlegger was viewed as providing an essential service. It was common knowledge that many of the "bootleg joints" were operated by women and many local lawmen were "paid off" to let these places operate.

The whiskey trade in the boomtowns, as well as bootlegging nationwide, was cutthroat business. It took tough men to handle deliveries, as it was not uncommon for loads of whiskey to be hijacked or stolen. This great frenzy became a breeding ground of modern-day gangsters, bank robbers, safe crackers and killers. It was a far cry from the old-time western outlaw. Even Al Spencer, bank robber and train robber, wanted nothing to do with the boomtown thugs. These were men who would kill for a price and it didn't need to be too high.

Why did Henry Grammar get into the whiskey business? Maggie was getting a hefty check for her headright every quarter. Maybe it was a challenge. He loved a challenge. Some have speculated that he did it to help a buddy or two to make some money. He helped some to set up stills, one on an island in the river, and bought the finished product and sold it to distributors. Because of his involvement, Grammer has been written up as "King of the Bootleggers".

Much of what happened in the years 1921 through 1923 must be viewed in hindsight. Thousands and thousands of words were published in newspapers across the nation. It made for fascinating reading. The old west was wild again. And when it was tagged: The Osage Reign of Terror, each rumor, each accusation was treated as fact.

Likewise, countless books have been published dealing with the same topic. From the beginning stories, which were printed as news items, contained errors. Unfortunately, some authors failed to research their material and have relied on error prone news reporters and the same errors have come across as fact. True, these errors may seem minor, but when viewed in the larger picture, they cry out for correction.

Agents from the Bureau of Investigation (later FBI) moved on the scene after the Osage Tribal Council petitioned Washington for help. In their attempt to enhance their reputation as an investigative agency, the agents were determined to "get" someone and it appeared the trail led to three men: W.K. Hale, a Fairfax banker, Earnest Burkhart, his nephew and John Ramsey, a farmhand. As these three, plus some lesser names, came to trial in 1926, the prosecution pulled out all stops.

As the investigation continued, the rumors grew and reporters from many papers added to the rumor mill. All the talk centered on Hale and his nephew, Earnest Burkhart.

During the months of investigation the Department of Justice furnished leaks to the newspapers causing them to be filled with stories based either on these leaks or pure speculation. The Federal men were especially active in the state prisons of Oklahoma and Kansas. Among the inmates from prisons who were brought to Guthrie as witnesses were Dick Gregg, John Mayo, John Gregg and Ralph White.

Charles Roff wrote: "It is interesting to note how many of the prosecution witnesses had been taken repeatedly out at night by these agents for "questioning". I was in Guthrie during the entire session of the jury, but was not called to appear, but I did have the opportunity to learn something of the operation of the Department of Justice. In early 1926, I was subpoenaed along with possibly one hundred others."

Prison inmates were promised lighter sentences or possibly freedom for their testimony. The investigators were willing to accept random testimony from prison inmates whose crimes ranged from bank robbery, hijacking, murder, fraud, bootlegging and gambling, to a whole roster of lesser crimes.

In an effort to "skip over the little guys to catch the big fish", Hale, John Ramsey and Earnest Burkhart were brought to trial. The trials became a legal imbroglio with many witnesses who were afraid to talk or lied under oath. In 1926, Earnest Burkhart was sentenced to life imprisonment in the Oklahoma State Penitentiary. In 1926, Hale and Ramsey were sentenced to life imprisonment at the Federal Penitentiary at Leavenworth. A final appeal was made by Hale in 1929 and was dismissed.

During these investigations, Henry Grammer's name was mentioned quite often, but Henry had long been dead. One of the prisoners called in to testify at the first trial was John Mayo who drove the car when Henry was killed.

Much was made of the fact that W.K. Hale was in Fort Worth, Texas, attending the Fat Stock Show and Rodeo at the time the Smith home was blown up in Fairfax, killing Bill Smith, his wife, Rita Kile Smith, and their white servant Nettie Brookshire.

Henry was a long time member of the Texas and Southwestern Cattleraisers Association and was often called on to judge their annual rodeos in Fort Worth. As for Hale's reason for being in Fort Worth at the same time could have been for any number of reasons.

One writer, who wrote extensively on the Osage murders, possibly saw a connection between the two men and kept writing about the Hale-Grammer ring. If these two men were "partners" in crime, Hale had his "partner" killed a short time later, in June 1923. Asa "Ace" Kirby, the person who set off the charge to blow up the Smith home was killed in June 1923 after Hale had him "set up" to burglarize a store. A shotgun blast tore him apart.

Many of the later day accusations against Grammer are completely out of character in how he is remembered today. Contrary to some accounts, Henry would never be part of a murder ring, bootlegger, yes, murder, no. One convict in the Oklahoma State Penitentiary said Henry went to Kansas City to look for a hit man to do some work on behalf of W. K. Hale. This was not logical as there were plenty of hit men in the oilfield boomtowns. No need to go to Kansas City and Henry would not have been a flunky for Hale. Another writer stated that Grammer had a long list of felonies, ranging from cattle rustling and bank robbery to cold-blooded murder. Some folks said he had the morals of a coyote in heat.

As for the bank robbery charge? The old chestnut was pulled out of the fire again and is based on a news account that Grammer was involved in the robbery of a Coffeyville, Kansas bank. The men who pulled the job entered the city in a covered wagon, pulled the robbery and then escaped on horseback into the Osage Hills. The newspaper reporter who made up that story failed to check with the Coffeyville authorities, as the last bank holdup in that community was pulled off by the Dalton gang in October 1892 and it was a disaster for them.

At the time of the robbery, Henry Grammer was still recovering from the stab wound he received in Burbank in 1915. It is true that he was recovering in an Arkansas City hospital.

All of this misinformation that has been printed over the years has only added to the Grammer mystic. As the grizzled old reporter said in the movie, <u>The Man Who Shot Liberty Valance:</u> "When the facts conflict with the legend, print the legend".

CROSSING THE
RUBICON

What really happened on the afternoon of June 14, 1923? Only one thing is certain: Henry Grammer lay dying in a dusty road outside of Shidler in the Burbank oilfield. Allegedly, death came from being thrown out of his Cadillac automobile, which had been driven at a high speed by a man named John Mayo. Henry was a passenger in the car along with Mayo's wife. At the time it was reported that neither of the Mayos were injured.

A Pawhuska newspaper described the scene: "In addition to a broken neck, Grammer's left side was torn out and the left side of his head smashed. Directly after the accident, the Mayos disappeared, but John Mayo was later apprehended by Henry Majors. No charge had been placed against him last night, but people from Webb City will be here this morning with something definite. When arrested, Mayo was drunk and had two large guns on his person."

Henry Grammer was larger than life and the manner in which he died set off a flood of rumors and conspiracy theories. One rumor, which was widely circulated, was that someone had tampered with the brakes on Henry's car causing it to crash. One story came out that Henry and John Mayo were in Webb City where, in a drunken rage, beat three men with their pistols. Fearing they had killed the men, Henry and Mayo drove wildly out of town. It was believed at the time they were headed out of the country as $10,000 was found on Henry's body. This money was to be used for their getaway.

One prominent rancher remembered his father talking about the accident that claimed Henry's life. "The dust had hardly settled when Deputy Sheriff Fred Whitaker came upon the wreck. He saw Mayo going through Henry's pockets. Mayo started to pull his gun, but Whitaker jammed his own gun in Mayo's belly stopping him."

Mayo was taken to Pawhuska and jailed where he was charged with manslaughter based on the evidence that he was driving the car at a high and dangerous speed while drunk. Later at his trial, his defense was that at the time of the accident he was sober, but after he and Grammer's body were taken into Shidler, he was so shook up and in such shock over the death of his friend, he got a pint of corn whiskey and drank it all at once, which resulted in his drunken condition at the time of his arrest. The jury believed him and he was acquitted.

John Mayo would be a major player in a few years in the government's investigation into the Osage Indian murders and was known to be an expert safe cracker.

Henry's fatal accident wasn't reported to County officials until around 10:00 p.m. that night. The undertaker at Shidler was preparing the body for burial and found a suspicious hole that looked as if it could be a bullet wound.

County Attorney Charles Roff would later say that no autopsy was performed and the hole, behind Grammer's shoulder did indeed look like a bullet hole, but could have been caused by a broken bone. No mention of the other wounds nor was the hole probed for a bullet. Case closed.

Roff considered W.K. Hale as a friend and supporter. When Roff first ran for Osage County Attorney, Hale helped him get elected.

"I still remember that night," said C.O. Leuschner. "I was just a kid, but I went to the Shidler Funeral Home with my mother, Irene and Aunt Maggie. Poor Aunt Maggie! She was consumed with grief and really didn't push for an

133

investigation. She couldn't believe Uncle Henry was dead.

"The family had a very low opinion of John Mayo and we always suspected that Hale had Henry killed. They had a falling out when Henry learned some things from John Ramsey, a farmhand for Henry. Ramsey showed up in a new car bought with money from Hale."

"I believe it was on the street at Burbank," said Walt Colby, "My father heard it. Henry cornered Hale there and Henry really chewed out that guy. When Henry got his anger up, he was an awesome sight. He had heard what was going on and he didn't like it and he didn't like his name being mentioned and if it didn't stop, he was going to do something about it. But you didn't threaten Hale and get away with it."

Even today, seventy-five years after Grammer's death, old-timers in Osage County still believe that Hale arranged for Henry to be killed because he knew too much. It was common knowledge that Henry often carried large sums of money on his person. Hale and Mayo knew this, so the alleged fight at Webb City was a setup. Somehow it was planned to have Henry shot or stabbed in the back, loaded into his car, and with Mayo driving, race out of town to a convenient spot, get out, leave Henry's body in the car and wreck it. Hard to explain how Mayo and his wife escaped injury.

Suppose Mayo was told that he could have all the cash money Grammer carried in his pockets, but this plan failed when Deputy Sheriff Whitaker happened on the accident.

"One peculiar thing about this accident," remembered Leuschner, "was that Uncle Henry never wanted anyone to drive his car but himself. The report said he was drunk. I'd ridden with him after he had been drinking and he never drove over twenty-five miles an hour. We would laugh about it."

Did Henry have a premonition concerning his own death? Hard to say. He never really got over the death of his brother Tom. "Tears would always come into his eyes when he got to reminiscing about Uncle Tom," said Leuschner.

Only a year earlier, Henry had been stunned when he learned of the death of his old roping buddy, Clay McGonagill, who had been killed when he came in contact with a high voltage

135

electric line.

A big advertisement appeared in the June 8, 1923 issue of THE OSAGE CHIEF (Fairfax) promoting space in the nearly completed mausoleum in the IOOF cemetery in Ponca City, Oklahoma. The interior had gleaming white marble lining every hallway. On a list of citizens buying space was the name of Henry Grammer.

Two weeks later Henry was dead!

"A bunch of us were at a rodeo in Wynona when we got word that Henry had been killed," said Red Carter. "Me, my brother Barton, Ben Johnson and Fred Beeson pulled out and went to see Maggie at the ranch. She asked us to take Henry's body to the river bridge at Kaw City. As it was a heavy steel coffin it was going to be a problem. The Arkansas River had been out of its banks and every creek and slough was standing in water. We made a cart out of some old cultivator wheels, put the coffin on it and started out. We pushed and pulled that cart through mud and water, but finally made it to the bridge. Why did we work so hard? Henry was our friend. He would have done the same for one of us. Don't believe everything written about him."

On June 15, 1923, THE PONCA CITY NEWS reported on funeral plans for Grammer: "Funeral services for Henry Grammar, (sic) Osage County rancher who was instantly killed in a motor car accident Thursday night, will be held at the Christian Church at 2 o'clock Sunday afternoon. Rev. E.C. Whitaker will officiate. Burial will be at the mausoleum. Motor cars will be on hand to accommodate friends and relatives from the Osage side."

"There were thousands of people at the funeral," said Leuschner. "Flowers arrived for three days. There were even people coming in by plane."

An article in the same issue of the paper confirmed this last statement: "Plane Falls With Poncans. Clarence Soldani, owner and pilot of an airplane, and C.H. Higdon, florist, were injured early this afternoon when the wing of the plane struck a fence as it was taking off in a field near the Henry Grammer home in Osage County. Both sustained cuts and bruises. They were brought to the Ponca City hospital via airplanes. The extent of their injuries had not been learned at this time.

"Soldani has been in the air from

morning until dark almost continuously since Sunday during the flood. He had planned to voyage to Dallas today to bring Lewis (sic) Grammer home to attend the funeral of his father."

The hearse carrying Henry's body was followed by a long, long procession of automobiles. After the casket was carried into the Grammer room, it was opened for viewing. Flowers overflowed every space up and down the hall.

As reported in the Ponca City Daily News: "Dewey, Okla.-- Some fitting ceremony will be arranged here on July 5, to commemorate the memory of Henry Grammer, once champion steer roper of the world, who was recently killed in an automobile accident in the Osage Nation. Grammer had visited every point in the United States, Canada and Mexico where rodeos are held and was known to every contestant in the world of cowboys and cowgirls. The Dewey Round-Up opens the morning of July 4 and an entry blank had been received from Grammar before his death. This is the fifteenth year of the Round-up and Grammar had missed but one contest here."

The Grammer room in the

Marble Halls is now full. Maggie was next to rest there in 1965, Henry, Jr., (Buster) in 1980, Tomasine Plomondon Rowe in 1981, and Zeke Plomondon, Tomasine's first husband. Louis died in 1980 and is buried in the Catholic section in the IOOF Cemetery. The Grammer children all died within one year of each other. With their passing, so passed the Grammer legacy, as there were no grandchildren.

C.O. said, "I remember Aunt Maggie as a sweet, gentle woman. After Uncle Henry died, people were always taking advantage of her. She once had a man come to the house and put new curtains over the windows. He charged her something like eight thousand dollars. Another time, two guys, whom she knew slightly, fed her a story about a man who used to work for Henry who lay dying in Colorado. They asked for money so this guy could have a proper burial. When this man later showed up at the ranch, alive and well, Maggie knew she had been lied to.

"Uncle Henry used to wear a gold medal which said "Champion Steer Roper," on it. He sometimes wore it on his coat lapel. I asked Tomasine about it, as I would liked to have had it as a memento, but she said it disappeared.

"Uncle Henry used to wear a beautiful diamond ring. Had it on when he was killed. Maggie later sold it at a fraction of its value. Remember, Uncle Henry provided the best for his family. He and Maggie drove Cadillacs. They dressed well, but the kids squandered their inheritance."

The site of the Grammer ranch is gone! Buried under the waters of Kaw Lake on the Arkansas River. Only the ghost of the legend remains. His picture still hangs on the walls of many Osage ranch houses. With pride, some point to a Henry Grammer saddle, Grammer spurs, a prison-made horsehair quirt or bridle. The mystique is still here!

One old-timer who knew Henry well said: "He was some hombre."

LETTER TO THE AUTHOR

FROM TOM BENBROOK

"I was just a boy when my folks moved into what was called "the bottoms" along the Arkansas River between Ponca City and Kaw City. Our cow pasture joined the Grammer pasture on the south. Right near the corner where the two places met was a still operated by Jim Ballew and I supposed he operated it for Henry Grammer. There have been stories about the size of moonshine whiskey stills being eight feet tall or better. Don't believe it. I saw plenty of stills all over Osage County and the average pot was five foot tall. The operator had to load them with buckets. Since they loaded them with buckets, anything taller would require a ladder which was hard carrying a bucket.

"There was a creek nearby where I often saw it run white with mash after the moonshine was taken off. Another still was on an island in the middle of the Arkansas River due north of our land. A man by the name of John Farrar ran it. It took fairly high water to cover the island for it was quite high. I reckon the big flood of 1923 got most of it. It was a Jim-dandy location as booze could be delivered both to Osage County on the east and Kay County on the west.

"There was not a still in that

county which all the neighbors did not know about, but we were all closed mouth. No snitches. I plainly remember the big raid when I was with my Dad and my older brother and we chanced to go by the Grammer place and saw all the raiders. Dad had my brother drive on up to Jim Ballew's place. A good road led right to it. We met Boss Powers before we got to the still and told him the law people were on a raid and Boss took out on a run to the still. It had 100 bbl of mash in it. It those days, we were a closed mouth neighborhood.

"We later learned that the raiders made a raid down on notorious Beal Street in Whizbang and confiscated beer, whiskey and narcotics.

"There were a good number of stills in the country along that old river bottom. We had a good neighbor by the name of Walt Hamilton who made a lot of the copper boilers and he was an expert at it.

"Much has been made of Grammer's reputation as the kingpin bootlegger during those boom days, maybe he was, but it hardly seems likely as there were a lot more people who were selling booze besides him. Not only was it coming in from other counties, but it also came from out of state. He was blamed for some things which were not his doing.

"Henry was a good neighbor and expected to be treated the same way. He didn't like to be pushed around. It was rumored that Henry had a hidden, trick door in his barn that could be opened with a hairpin. This is not true. I grew up with Buster (Henry, Jr.) and we always played in the barn and there was no trick door.

"Mrs. Grammer was a wonderful woman. She never tired of talking about Henry. I heard her tell my father that John Mayo killed Henry. Henry had a bullet hole in his back. She once took the two Grammer boys and me to the rodeo in Cheyenne where she mixed with some of her old rodeo friends. We boys got to ride horses all the time we were there."

EPILOGUE

The more I study the past, the more I am convinced that too often man has been guilty of judging people and events of the past by present standards and not by the way things were at the time they occurred. The road to marble halls was not easy.

Bill Beaty remembers his grandfather Pitts Beaty, once a mayor of Fairfax, Oklahoma, as being close to Henry Grammer and often spoke of him in the most glowing terms. Never a negative word.

Honored as being one of the pioneers of early day rodeo, Henry Grammer was inducted into the Rodeo Hall of Fame on October 22, 2000. The ceremony was held at a banquet at the National Cowboy Hall of Fame and Western Heritage Center in Oklahoma City.

About the Author

Arthur Shoemaker is a native of Laredo, Texas. After college and serving in the 8th Air Force during WWII, he worked in the oil patch across Oklahoma and Kansas. He and his wife Peggy have been married for over 50 years.

He is a member of the Western Writers of America and the Rodeo Historical Society. He has been published in True West, Old West, Civil War Times, Tombstone Epitaph, Persimmon Hill, The Ketch Pen, Wild West, Oklahoma Today and the Chronicles of Oklahoma. His latest book Railroading Through the Osage Hills was acclaimed. Arthur has had over three hundred book reviews in the Tulsa World. He and Peggy reside in Hominy, Oklahoma.